Teaching at College and University

Teaching at College and University

Effective Strategies and Key Principles

Sarah Moore, Gary Walsh and Angélica Rísquez

 Open University Press

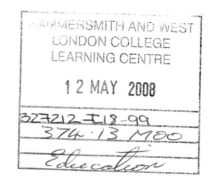
Open University Press
McGraw-Hill Education
McGraw-Hill House
Shoppenhangers Road
Maidenhead
Berkshire
England
SL6 2QL

email: enquiries@openup.co.uk
world wide web: www.openup.co.uk

and Two Penn Plaza, New York, NY 10121-2289, USA

First published 2007

A catalogue record of this book is available from the British Library

ISBN-10: 0 335 22109 2 (pb)   0 335 22110 6 (hb)
ISBN-13: 987 0 335 22109 7 (pb)   987 0 335 22110 3 (hb)

Library of Congress Cataloguing-in-Publication Data
CIP data applied for

Typeset by RefineCatch Limited, Bungay, Suffolk
Printed in Poland by OZGraf S.A.
www.polskabook.pl

The *McGraw·Hill* Companies

For Ger, Nancy and Maurice

Contents

Acknowledgements

We are very grateful to the following colleagues and friends for the teaching and learning-related inputs, support and encouragement they provided while this book was being written: Maura Murphy and Nyiel Kuol at the University of Limerick's Centre for Teaching and Learning; Anne O'Keeffe and Geraldine Brosnan at the Learner Support unit at MIC; Maria Hinfelaar and Terry Twomey at Limerick Institute of Technology; Don Barry, John O'Donoghue; Catherine Jeanneau, Caroline Graham, Angela Chambers and George McClelland all leaders and advocates of the establishment of UL's discipline-specific learner support units; Geraldine O'Neill and Terry Barrett in the Centre for Teaching and Learning at University College Dublin, Jean Hughes at the Centre for Teaching and Learning in Dublin City University, Betty Jane Punnett at the University of the West Indies in Barbados, Harriet Cotter of Third Level Provision, Co. Clare, Karen Young at University College Galway, Rowena Murray at the University of Strathclyde and Morag Thow at Glasgow Caledonian University. Each has been a role model for creating and sustaining positive, empowering, innovative educational strategies and we feel fortunate to have benefited from their commitment and collegiality.

Para Sebastián Risquez y Crescen Lopez por su amor incondicional.

Also warm thanks to Elizabeth and Paul Moore – extraordinary teachers of many important life lessons, and to Michael O'Dea – this book was his idea. Finally, we acknowledge Betty O'Dea (1911–2006), an inspiring and committed teacher from whom many generations of children learned the empowering principles of enthusiasm, optimism and engagement.

Introduction

Academic teachers face a range of competing pressures and tasks as part of their professional lives. In this context, we believe that there is room for teachers to consider approaches that provide simple ideas for enhancing competence, reducing stress, increasing enjoyment and for helping them to teach with pleasure and satisfaction.

This book contains a collection of advice that we hope will provide practical, thoughtful and actionable ideas to support your teaching. The strategies and tactics that are presented together provide a positive, empowered approach to teaching at university and college.

We have designed this book to be of particular use to new teachers, especially those who do not have specialist backgrounds in education, pedagogy or academic practice. We introduce theory and literature from the fields of organizational behaviour, learning, pedagogy and education, but in ways that we hope do not undermine or interfere with the very practical focus that we have attempted to adopt.

We provide a range of evidence-based insights that will help support teaching and the delivery of academic expertise both within and beyond classroom settings. The sections and themes that this book contains can be used by academics from any discipline as a backdrop to their teaching. When planning and thinking about teaching, its contents can help you adopt a reflective orientation, but also simply to try out different classroom, interactive or discursive activities and tactics that other people have found useful in similar kinds of settings.

We focus on helping you to develop effective skills in conventional classroom settings (such as lecture halls, tutorial rooms and in one-to-one student consultations) and we also include a series of ideas and orientations that will help with teaching using on-line, blended approaches or in distance education environments.

Outline

Each of the major subsections of this book reflects a separate theme that has been shown to influence teaching competence. All of them, as you will see, are interlinked. We know that the best teachers in almost all contexts are those who are self-aware, and who understand the ways in which their presence and their behaviour impact on the responses of their students (Price 2006). This is a key theme that we focus on in Chapter 1.

In Chapter 2, we outline and discuss a range of key, basic skills that need to be mastered in most further and higher educational teaching contexts. We know that such skills need to be acquired and developed quite quickly – sometimes without much institutional support or advice. These include skills that often they don't get briefed about in focused, actionable and digestable ways at the times that they are most needed (Boice 2000). Chapter 2 covers such practical issues as preparing for a class, delivery techniques, assessment decisions, curriculum design and communication skills.

Good teachers find simple ways to focus on their students as well as on their subjects (see, for example, Chickering and Gamson 1987). Some teachers do this in ways that might first appear impossible, particularly when they are teaching to very large groups. We explore many of these tactics and suggest how you might experiment with them in your own teaching in Chapter 3.

Chapter 4 helps to explore how coping with orientations towards technology in teaching can be confidently handled by teachers from all disciplines and backgrounds.

In Chapter 5 we apply some established principles associated with time management, organizational awareness and assertiveness to help you manage the often contradictory pressures of life in higher and further educational settings.

In Chapter 6 we provide insights and considerations that focus on the often thorny issue of assessment and examination, and highlight the simple principles that can help guide your assessment strategy as a teacher.

Chapter 7 focuses on helping you to find ways of taking good physical, emotional and professional care of yourself, something we have found that university and college teachers don't always prioritize (Chandler et al. 2002; Acker and Armenti 2004). We explore how staying physically and emotionally healthy is not just intrinsically good for you, but also encourage you to consider how it can enhance your performance and your success as a teacher and an academic.

You can use this book to dip into and out of – the advice it contains does not necessarily need to be accessed in any particular order. You may find that at different stages in your teaching, or at different times in each semester, you need different kinds of advice, and so scanning the contents for issues that are relevant to you at a particular point in time may be an appropriate, timely and useful way to use this book.

This is a practical guide to teaching in further and higher educational environments. If you are enrolled on a programme for accrediting your own teaching, it might provide useful signposts to pedagogical, learning and educational literature that could be helpful as part of that process. However, if you are not currently seeking accreditation, it is a useful text to supplement, enhance and develop your approaches to teaching within your discipline.

In writing this book we have aimed to provide a straightforward, multi-level, practical guide from which we hope you will be able to derive a range of simple and actionable teaching-related benefits.

1

Developing your self-awareness as a teacher

Introduction • Tapping into your natural ability to communicate • Knowing what your students think of you • Getting ready to respond to student views and feelings about your teaching • Developing your repertoire of responses to feedback on your teaching • Helping your institution to use student evaluations responsibly • Looking at yourself on video • Talking to others about your teaching • Watching other people teach • Getting peers to observe your teaching • Keeping a teaching diary • Having an academic mentor • Building your sense of entitlement as a teacher and scholar • Avoiding professional jealousy • Recognizing the power that comes with teaching • Revelling in the clandestine • Knowing your mystery ingredient

Introduction

Teachers need to know themselves. The benefits of understanding and reflecting on the impact that they have on their students are well documented (e.g., Brookfield 1995). The following sections explore evidence and give advice that can help you to develop your pedagogical self-awareness. All of these strategies are underpinned by the assertion that knowing your students' views of you, and understanding how they react to your teaching styles and strategies can provide you with invaluable information and ideas for enhancing your teaching, particularly when analysed with the assistance of trusted peers and mentors.

1.1 Tapping into your natural ability to communicate

- Simple features of communication are useful guidelines for teaching.
- Good communication involves: attracting attention, ensuring clarity and comprehension and building in opportunities for feedback.
- Creating a climate for 'constructive interruption' can enhance classroom communication and clarity.

As a teacher, your ability to communicate is essential to your capacity to help people learn. It is not just your command of your subject (which is of course very important) but it is your ability to make connections with others and to transmit ideas that will really bring your subject alive. One of the interesting paradoxes in educational contexts is that the more experienced you become, the harder it can sometimes be to communicate effectively with new students (e.g., Moore and Kuol 2005). This is at least partly because the more familiar you become with your topic and your subjects, the harder it is to see that material through the eyes of novice learners (Abbas and McClean 2003).

In order to become (and more importantly to stay) good at teaching, you need constantly to remind yourself of the simple principles associated with effective communication. This is a good way of keeping your teaching approach fresh and focused, and of reminding yourself of the essential ways in which you're trying to help your students to learn.

As you plan to teach, think of yourself as the source of an important series of messages. Plan to encode those messages using language, images, ideas and metaphors that your students will understand. Deliver your message in a way that will help capture their attention, maximize their chances of understanding, believing in and remembering what you are teaching. As you do this, check regularly if your students are still engaged, if they still 'get it', if they are still with you, absorbing and learning the material that you are bringing to them.

In developing your confidence as a teacher, remember that you probably communicate with great effect in many other challenging contexts. Teaching contains important similarities with any situation in which people need to communicate with one another and to achieve particular goals associated with that communication.

Many of the features of good conversation are also the features of good teaching. All participants in the conversation need to feel engaged and empowered (even if one person talks more than everyone else, as is often the case in large group settings). Everyone needs to have at least some command over the langage that is being used, and where they don't, efforts need to be made to help develop that language.

To have a satisfactory conversation, you need to avoid making the assumption that everyone shares the same amount of knowledge or understands the same principles and concepts. This may seem like common sense to you. However, there is a common phenomenon among teachers, and that is the unwitting use of language or words that students simply do not understand – and because it's unwitting, it's often difficult to guard against.

You can make sure that your students understand the words and concepts that you are teaching by creating a norm within your class – inviting students to signal to you any time when you have used a word, phrase or explanation that they do not understand. Simple teaching tactics can formalize this norm by providing active and endorsed permission to students to call a halt to your teaching when they are finding things incomprehensible. You could try installing techniques and tricks within your own classroom settings that don't just allow interruptions, but positively encourage them under defined circumstances. Students really do like it when they are given a formal way to signal any lack of understanding. With your encouragement (perhaps by handing out red stop signs, or by writing a list of groundrules that define 'constructive interruption') and when they get over an initial reluctance to draw attention to themselves, constructive interruption can gradually become a much-appreciated way for them to initiate and enhance classroom discussion (see also Chapter 2, section 2.6).

Clear communication norms encourage students to communicate with you as well as providing useful signs when it's time for you to try to communicate more effectively with them. In addition, it creates a situation in which they become more active learners – scanning the material that you are teaching and being on their guard to keep making sure they understand.

Think carefully about ways in which you can adapt your capacity to communicate in all the classroom situations you face in order to enhance your teaching and to enrich your students' learning.

1.2 Knowing what your students think of you

- Aim to adopt simple, time-efficient techniques for regularly gathering students' views about your teaching and their learning.
- Treat student responses as a powerful personal resource.
- Consider student views openly and non-defensively in ways that support your effectiveness as a teacher.

Most people can recall or identify teachers who are somehow resented by their students without seeming either to know or to care. The extent to which teachers can be oblivious or impervious to the views of their students does vary. Some are hypersensitive to student views, while others are perhaps completely unconcerned about them. We argue that as a teacher of college or university students, it is useful to have a good idea of what your students think of you. The more accurate this idea is, the better for everyone. Faculty often speak of their amazement the first time they read a student evaluation report, having had no idea how positively (or negatively) they or some aspects of what they do were viewed by students. Information about what your students think of you can be a powerful personal resource.

We are not always encouraged to seek this kind of information, and even if we are, it is not necessarily used to support our professional development. Understanding the kinds of perceptions and reactions that you produce in your students is something that can empower and equip you with ideas about improving your teaching, interacting more effectively with your students and generally being in control of what you do. You do, however, sometimes need to brace yourself when looking for honest feedback. It can be a humbling experience. And you need to develop an undefensiveness about how students express these perceptions in order to make the most of them in how you react and respond to them.

There are many ways in which you can attempt to get an honest idea of your students' experiences of your teaching. Some of these are things that you will initiate yourself, others may be available through services provided by your own institution. And when using the services of a central resource like a centre for teaching and learning, you need to make your own decisions about the quality and trustworthiness of the processes in place.

We recommend the following kinds of simple techniques for getting a better view of your students' attitudes towards your teaching:

1 *End of lecture paragraphs*: Ask your students to write for 5 minutes about their views on the best and worst aspects of your lecture. Have them hand in their reflective written pieces and review the comments. This simple activity can very quickly give you a picture of what your students have taken away from the lecture, as well as ideas about how you might be able to enhance their experience in the future.

2 *Classroom-based focus groups*: These are slightly more elaborate ways of getting structured feedback from students about their views on your teaching. Have someone facilitate a short (15 minute) discussion at the end of your lecture or at a key time during the semester and collect the main views, focusing in particular on areas in which you feel you know least about students' reactions and experiences.

3 *Specific issue surveys*: Distribute specific-issue survey questionnaires if you want to find out more about students' experiences of particular aspects of

the course, library resources, the main course textbook, in-class exercises, assignments or exams.

4 *Informal conversations*: Join your students after a lecture occasionally in order to debrief and get their opinions and reactions; or find other informal ways of having honest one-to-one interactions with students.

The closer you are to knowing their opinions and experiences, the better equipped you will be to respond appropriately to the issues that arise. It might sound like a lot of extra work, and indeed seeking out this kind of information does take time, energy and at least a certain degree of humility. But the effort that it takes to gather this kind of information can save a lot of time and trouble in the longer term, particularly if there are problems with your students' capacity and orientation towards learning the subjects you are trying to teach.

Be reflective and don't panic. Students do sometimes say dramatic things if you give them the space to do so. If you ask them honestly for their views, you do risk hearing things like: 'I hate this topic'; 'I'm completely lost'; 'This is so boring' and other discouraging sentiments. You'll also hear some great endorsements too. Try to disentangle their views of you from their ideas about the subject you teach and the challenges that you have created for them. Don't shy away from listening to and responding appropriately to their views.

1.3 Getting ready to respond to student views and feelings about your teaching

- Recognize the potentially emotional impact that student feedback can have on you.
- Work to interpret student feedback in reasonable, positive and action-orientated ways.
- Utilize student feedback where it clearly provides guidelines for enhancing teaching and learning.

Even when university teachers are active in gathering student views, they don't always have firm habits associated with receiving and following through on them. We tend not to be prepared to react positively or appropriately to this kind of data. Many of us have difficulty even knowing how to start to interpret the data which student surveys produce.

While teachers do tend to get feedback increasingly regularly either through their own student surveys or through the 'quick tick' types of questionnaires distributed and analysed centrally, it seems now that feedback fatigue is starting to become prevalent among students who are increasingly frequently being asked for their opinions of and reactions to teaching. One of the main reasons for feedback fatigue is based on the perception that systems for gathering student feedback are often used as shallow instruments, designed to satisfy relatively unsubstantial bureaucratic requirements associated with an increasing preoccupation with institutional control and measurement rather than a source of positive dialogue between teachers and learners (Johnson 2000). If this is the case in your teaching context, then it won't take very long before your students learn this too (that is if they haven't already) – and start to respond superficially, infrequently or not at all to requests for feedback on your teaching.

One of the ways to continue to receive constructive and valid views from your students, whether through structured questionnaires, informal conversations or semi-structured focus groups, is to commit to responding to these views in some meaningful way – to promise students that you will register what they have said, and to undertake to respond in positive ways to the information that they provide. However, it is not always easy to respond meaningfully to student feedback. It can, for example, be very difficult to encounter and respond to student feedback that is either negative or surprising (or both). Indeed when you combine the characteristics of negativity and surprise, you get a sometimes toxic cocktail of information that instead of motivating you to enhance and develop your approach, can lead to dismay, dejection, disappointment, defensiveness and denial (see Ilgen and Davis 2000).

Studies have concluded that the emotional impact on faculty who receive student evaluation reports should not be underestimated (see, for example, Moore and Kuol 2005). Indeed it is the emotional dimension of this experience that usually requires most attention. Individual faculty and their mentors could help to understand defensive or stress-related reactions better if they explored their own predictions of feedback in advance of the receipt of feedback from students. A system whereby faculty rate their own teaching in advance of students' efforts to do the same might help to equip them with greater insights into how different kinds of feedback might affect them and in what ways.

While student evaluations of teaching (SETs) have been in operation for many years in many different contexts, much less effort has been applied to the development of an approach to feedback reaction that enhances the likelihood that SETs will be used appropriately, constructively and in the interests of learning. This can only serve to confirm Johnson's (2000) and our own fears that these systems tend to serve the shallow needs of educational bureaucracy and not the deeper needs of learning and teaching in higher educational contexts.

Carson (2001) argues that teachers may need to be shielded from unhelpful or damaging feedback, and that feedback that is perceived to be non-specific, unactionable, irrelevant or in some other way outside the teacher's control, can damage a sense of professional empowerment as well as subsequent efforts to teach effectively. However, you may also need help in working out how to be responsive to reasonable feedback from your students, especially if you feel under fire and criticized, even when the feedback does direct you to possible areas for improvement.

Depending on whether the feedback is largely positive or negative, and whether it is broadly surprising or unsurprising, feedback reactions and responses may tend to be characterized in different ways, reflecting different levels of commitment to enhancing and changing teaching activity and orientation. When we studied the responses of teachers to different types of feedback, this is what we found:

1 *Where feedback is positive and expected*: Reactors seem to identify mild to moderate satisfaction indicating a positive but not urgent orientation to enhancing or sustaining the quality of their teaching.
2 *Where feedback is negative and expected*: We found strong tendencies to externalize responsibility for the feedback in a qualitative analysis of reactions in this category. Attributing problems to the challenges of the subject being taught is a common response, which may or may not be reflected in reality. Readiness to respond and repair teaching approaches that students are critical of was found in some but not all responders in this category.
3 *Where feedback is positive and unexpected*: Strongly emotional reactions were found in this category. Responders reacted extremely positively when feedback caused them to identify areas of teaching excellence or student appreciation of which they were not aware. Some potential evidence of stress (relating to the challenges of maintaining the positive views they had received) and some evidence of complacency seem to be evident among this category of responders.
4 *Where feedback is negative and unexpected*: Strong evidence of defensive cognitive dissonance was found in the responses to this type of student feedback. Denying, confronting and questioning the results were all evidenced in the articulated responses analysed. Fears and concerns about professional reputation emerged and self-affirmation activity was also in evidence. One respondent referred to their research-related strengths, possibly as a way of defusing their articulated sense of dismay with negative student feedback.

If you plan to get structured feedback from your students then it's also worthwhile to think about your own possible reactions and orientations yourself. Evidence suggests that it pays to prepare for the receipt of student feedback and orientate yourself more actively towards the possibility that some of this feedback may be surprising, negative or both (Moore and Kuol 2005).

We propose that based on the reactions that we have observed in some of our own teaching contexts, the guidelines presented in the next section might be useful in the development of healthy, functional, learning-orientated responses to student feedback.

1.4 Developing your repertoire of responses to feedback on your teaching

- Remember that both positive and negative feedback can emerge for reasons that do not always relate to the quality of your teaching.
- You don't have to respond to every specific aspect of student feedback.
- It's particularly useful to interrogate feedback that is in some way puzzling or surprising.
- Talking to students about the feedback they have given you can be a positive way of building rapport.

From our observations of different kinds of feedback reaction, we present six guidelines for faculty and their mentors when confronting student feedback:

1 Control your defence mechanisms. Ask yourself; what kinds of reactions am I having to this feedback and how is it likely to make me respond to my teaching challenges in the future? Whether your reactions are making you feel angry, euphoric, dismayed or pleased, analyse how these feelings might interfere with (or enhance) your capacity to develop an effective teaching strategy.

2 Particularly for puzzling feedback, try to get more information about the nature of your students' perceptions. As we have suggested, conducting follow-up focus groups, having informal discussions with student representatives or small student groups and distributing more specific questionnaires or feedback from peer observers are all strategies that you could use to find out more about an identified problem articulated in student feedback data (see also section 1.2).

3 Guard against overreaction to student feedback. We have found that it is very common for teaching faculty to fixate on one or two critical comments in feedback data that was overall extremely positive. This hypersensitivity may lead to reactions that only focus on minority or unrepresentative views. This risks reversing or undermining teaching strategies that are satisfactory for the majority of learners in a particular context.

4 Guard against under-reacting to student feedback. Student feedback that is extremely positive may yield complacent reactions and can be interpreted to mean that an individual's teaching strategy requires no further attention. Teaching effectiveness can vary from day to day, and from year to year. Different types of students experience the same kind of teaching in quite different ways. Assuming that one positive student feedback report means that you have 'got it right' for all time, is probably a mistake. Analyse positive feedback in ways that help you deliberately to exploit the strategies that

gave rise to it. But similarly, don't withdraw from negative feedback which can contain the potential for sometimes dramatic improvement. Negative feedback can cause faculty almost to recoil from their teaching responsibilities, and can lead them to focus instead on other aspects of their professional lives that affirm and endorse their sense of competence. But if you are to make negative feedback useful, it is worth paying attention to it and responding in appropriate and positive ways whenever this feels possible.

5 Use the feedback as a way of enhancing communication between you and your students, not bypassing it. Often, SETs are administered and collected via a central service. Many faculty do not discuss, or even mention, the survey either before or after its distribution. An effective SET system should be an aid to, not a replacement of, student–teacher communication. If you have some dialogue with your students about the nature of the SET survey, and the kinds of feedback you would find most useful and constructive, then you are more likely to receive constructive responses. Additionally, if you ensure that at some point after analysing the feedback you summarize the main issues that students raised (both positive and negative), you can engage in a more reasonable approach to the management of their expectations. Post-feedback dialogue with students might start by focusing on a particular issue raised by a large number of students. For example: 'I know you think the textbook is very hard work, but these are the reasons that I have prescribed it . . . And these are the things I'll try to do to help you navigate it'. Or the dialogue might be more generic, registering with students the overall tone of their feedback. For example: 'most of you feel quite comfortable with how the topics are unfolding so far but you seem to have some concerns about . . . and . . .' or: 'many of you are finding this course tough going – It's great that you told me this, because here are some of the things we can do together to address the challenges that you're facing'. Whatever strategy you adopt, it pays to talk directly to your students about their evaluations of your teaching. It helps to show them that you value their input and are likely to respond in some affirmative way to at least some of the issues that they raise. Sometimes, simply registering that you understand the students' struggles and signalling that you are prepared to help can turn negative student feeback around in ways that are positive both for you and for them.

6 Do not inevitably assume that positive student feedback necessarily indicates excellent teaching or that negative student feedback necessarily indicates poor teaching. Even though responding to students' ratings of your teaching can help to improve their perceptions of their learning environment, it is not always the appropriate thing to do. Some challenging experiences that students resist, may indeed be a necessary part of their learning journey, and may explain why some disciplines tend to receive more negative SETs than others. It always pays to put student feedback in context. As the literature has shown, class size, student maturity, type of

subject and timing of the feedback may all moderate or enhance your ratings (Cohen 1981; Feldman 1984; Kierstead et al. 1988; Cashin 1990a, 1990b).

1.5 Helping your institution to use student evaluations responsibly

- SET systems are more useful if they are well resourced and supported by follow-up coaching and assistance, particularly where negative feedback has been received.
- It is important to interpret student evaluation data firmly within the context it was gathered. Class size, time of year, student group and discipline need to be considered as part of that interpretation.

The literature in the field of student evaluations suggests strongly that systems for gathering student feedback should be accompanied by an institutional health warning. From an institutional perspective, systems that gather student evaluations must be underpinned by a sound orientation towards the information that it yields and the responses to which it gives rise (Olivares 2003). Assess your institution's treatment of student evaluation systems against the following institutional guidelines:

- SET systems need to be appropriately resourced as part of an integrated strategy that values and is prepared to respond positively to the voices of students, while also recognizing the potential for feedback from students that is not related to teacher performance.
- A SET system that is isolated and decontextualized may be neither a valid nor a reliable indicator of teacher performance. This can lead to the generation of performance-related data that is inherently threatening, unhelpful and stressful.
- Where SET data is valid and can help to point to problems with teaching, it still may not have a positive impact without the existence of the necessary supports to help overcome identified deficiencies in teaching performance.
- Given the emotional impact that SETs can have even when the system is voluntary and confidential, we believe that it is essential for institutions to provide support to help faculty interpret and respond healthily to the feedback that they get from students.
- A well resourced SET system that gives rise to learning supportive outcomes needs also to be accompanied by a culture of respectful feedback in student and faculty evaluations of one another. A well supported and managed SET

system may actually be able to introduce or reinforce a culture of reciprocal respect in higher education environments.

- Our experience suggests that it is extremely divisive, unhelpful and invalid to use SETs as league tables that pit different subjects, disciplines and teachers against one another. Data should be robust enough to help teachers compare their performance not against all other rated teachers, but rather all other rated teachers within similar categories (subject, class size and timing should all be taken into account). Otherwise, comparisons are not meaningful and can lead to unrealistically positive or negative self-evaluations.

- It is essential to take timing of SET surveys into account. Whether SET surveys are conducted early or late in the semester, before or after grades have been received, or at crucial stages in the unfolding of a taught programme can all have fundamental effects on the ways in which students respond. Surveys typically only tell a skeletal, snapshot story. Carrying out the same survey at several stages in the development of a particular module may help to interpret student experiences more comprehensively, but may also lead to the unwanted outcomes associated with feedback fatigue among students.

- In supporting and utilizing the potential benefits of a SET system, it may also be worthwhile to introduce a facility for getting faculty to predict their students' ratings in advance of collecting feedback. This information could equip coaches and educational developers with a 'diagnostic' of likely responses and enable constructive conversations with faculty, orientating them towards an appropriate teaching enhancement strategy.

1.6 Looking at yourself on video

- Video/DVD records of your teaching can be a useful professional development resource.
- Analyse footage of your teaching in structured and prompted ways by asking key questions.
- Performative dimensions of your teaching are important to be aware of, but are supported by a range of other skills that video footage may not reveal.

'Watching a videotape of yourself is an extremely valuable experience. Videotaping allows you to view and listen to the class as your students do; you can also scrutinize your students' reactions and responses to your teaching. By analyzing a videotape of the dynamics in your classroom, you can check the accuracy of your perceptions of how well you teach . . . identify those techniques that work and those that need revamping.'

(Gross-Davis 1993: 34)

Undertaking to look at yourself through other people's eyes is a revealing and sometimes disturbing exercise. But this information can also be extremely useful in your efforts to enhance and develop your teaching. In the short-term, seeing yourself on video can make you extremely self-conscious and uncertain, but in the medium- and longer-term, it can equip you with perspectives that genuinely help you to build on your strengtht, address weaknesses and to understand how your messages, ideas and instructions are conveyed to learners.

And if at first you can only look at yourself through your fingers, cringing at every hesitation or error, you will find gradually and with regular viewings that your external self becomes more tolerable, and that you can cast a more objective and favourable eye over your performance and delivery within the classroom. Looking at yourself on video is a true and brave commitment to enhancing your self-awareness.

Having a structured framework or checklist for analysing yourself is also useful. Categorize your observations of yourself under different headings. Look at your body language. How is your eye contact? What kind of presence do you feel you have? Are you at a physical distance from your students? How do you connect with them non-verbally? How do you use your hands? What kinds of gestures do you repeat? Do you have any repetitive verbal or non-verbal habits that you were previously unaware of and that might be distracting or confusing for your students? How does your voice sound? What does your overall tone communicate? What effect do these things seem to be having on your students?

These subtle aspects of your teaching may not be something you are aware of unless you see yourself from your students' perspective. You can also become more objective about other aspects of your teaching by viewing video footage. Focus on issues of pacing, clarity, transition from one topic to another, ways of engaging students and techniques you use to get them to interact. You can analyse student reactions too, if the video recording captures them as well as you in action (Acheson 1981).

Video analysis of your teaching is inevitably restricted to the performative aspects of your teaching. Nevertheless, watching yourself teach may give useful insights and strategies for enhancing essential aspects of your approach and your style.

1.7 Talking to others about your teaching

- You can address a lot of nagging fears or doubts about your teaching by talking to others about your strategies and style.
- It is helpful to treat teaching as a public rather than a private activity, which can benefit from the inputs and ideas of other teachers.

Strathern (1997) talks about teachers in current educational environments experiencing 'a vague, persistent and crippling sense of faliure' (p. 318). He attributes this mainly to the squeeze that is increasingly being applied to the time that teachers have to formulate, reformulate, make sense of and respond to their own reflections on their teaching and its impact.

It is easy to experience some perception of failure as a teacher. Your impact is not always easy to guage and it is often difficult to get accurate insights into your performance and your effectiveness. Teachers often say that they feel isolated and unsupported in some of their most important professional activities. Even though teaching is a very public act, particularly if you have large numbers of students, you may feel forced to treat it in paradoxically private ways. The public act of teaching risks becoming subverted into a private, lone act that is neither nourished nor criticized by other voices.

Expert teachers, experienced tutors, researchers and investigators who operate both within and outside your own discipline can have a powerful impact on your approach to teaching. But they are unlikely to do this unless you talk to them about your approaches, your mistakes, what you are planning and what you have already achieved. Have a look at some of the structured advice on mentoring in sections 1.9 and 1.11. It really does help to talk to others about your teaching plans, approaches, strategies and challenges. It is useful to set up your work schedule in a way that facilitates these kinds of conversations.

1.8 Watching other people teach

- At any stage in your teaching career it can be professionally refreshing to watch someone else teach.
- Climates in which teachers regularly attend each others' lectures/classes tend to be characterized by more active, effective teaching and learning dynamics.

Many of us have not attended lectures since we were students ourselves. We don't get the opportunity to sharpen our own approach because we don't get to see how much better or how much worse we might be. Your professional development as a teacher is likely to be dramatically enhanced if you can understand your approach, your delivery and your material in the context of the approaches and deliveries of other academics.

A useful and professionally developing habit you can adopt as a teacher is regular attendance at teaching sessions led by other people. In fact in environments where this is the norm, you're probably more likely to find cooperative, open and satisfying learning and teaching environments from the perspectives of both students and teachers. Local teaching climates may facilitate or prohibit this practice – but even where it is not the norm, you can create your own micro-climate and develop a system where a 'community of practice' can emerge among small clusters of committed teachers.

Asking permission to go to a lecture may take you or the person you are asking outside of the normal comfort zone. But the reciprocal professional benefits are already clear (Wiske et al. 2002). And enhancing academic teaching climates may involve creating norms that allow you into other teaching spaces and inviting others to do the same.

1.9 Getting peers to observe your teaching

- Peer observation is another potentially useful tool for teaching development.
- Assiduous and focused peer observation preparation can guide observations and ensure that they are as effective as possible.
- Peer observation is best conducted in a voluntary, supportive and collegiate environment.

Peer observation is quite a common and widespread approach to professional development in teaching in higher education (see for example Cosh 1998 and Allen 2002). Some of the problems and difficulties that we have highlighted relating to student feedback can be moderated by a good, trusted, thoughtful colleague who simply watches you teach and tells you what they think.

There are useful frameworks and provisos to consider whenever you decide or are required to invite someone into your classroom with the aim of helping you to improve or develop your teaching. Peer observation can be used as part of a system for accounting for and demonstrating a commitment to quality, thus satisfying the managerial requirements that increasingly exist in higher educational environments. But probably more importantly, from the point of view of individual teachers, and if negotiated well, peer observation can provide a fresh orientation on teaching, on student reaction and engagement, on subject delivery and on all sorts of subtle dimensions of teaching that teachers might otherwise be unaware of (see, for example, Hammersley-Fletcher and Orsmond 2004).

When planning to have your teaching observed, consider the more fine grained aims and objectives that are relevant to your own context, experience and focus as a teacher. Here are some suggestions about the aims of peer observations provided by Martin and Double (1998):

Aims associated with peer observation of teaching

- To help teachers to be more explicitly aware of their own personal approaches to the delivery of their subject in the context of a defined curriculum.
- To help teachers to consider enhancing and/or extending teaching techniques and styles, simply by considering and exploring new options with someone who has observed their teaching.
- To consider the interpersonal skills of the teacher through the ways in which teaching is delivered within a real setting.
- To help teachers become more practised in evaluating and appraising themselves.
- To use classroom observation reflections as the starting point for a discussion on curriculum planning and to develop curriculum planning skills.
- To pinpoint areas of teaching and expertise that are particularly strong or in particular need of enhancement or development.

(Adapted from Martin and Double 1998)

When planning to have your teaching observed by a peer, look at the above list of objectives and decide which of them is most relevant to you. Which objectives are closest to your own teaching enhancement goals? Which of them could help you to clarify creeping concerns you might have about your skills and orientations?

As a first step, standard practice in peer observation processes tend to involve a pre-observation meeting in which you and your peer discuss your aims, concerns and the kind of advice or observation you think might be most useful for you. It is a good idea if the observation itself is guided by broad structures which can help your peer observer to capture and provide useful and appropriate observations about your teaching and your students' learning. Common advice about post-observation meetings suggests that it is a good idea to meet as soon as possible after the observation has taken place (Martin and Double 1998), that peers should be prepared to deliver criticism as honestly and as constructively as possible (Morss and Murray 2005) and that written summaries of the feedback be clear, actionable and accurate, helping to identify the observers' perceptions of strengths as well as areas for development (Hansen and Liu 2005).

In our own experience, teachers generally find peer observation useful, professionally endorsing and worthwhile. However, there are caveats. Your peer may overpraise you when in fact you could do with a bit of well reasoned criticism. Your peer observer might be highly critical and undermining of something that is in fact having a positive effect on students' learning.

There may be other reasons why peer observation of feedback might not work. We suppose that this is a hazard in any situation where interaction and professional feedback from one colleague to another takes place. Nevertheless many teachers have made excellent strides forward in their teaching styles and impact through peer observation (Blackwell and McClean 1996).

You can maximize the benefits and avoid the pitfalls of peer observation of teaching by: choosing your peer carefully, preparing your peer for the session and giving them as much useful information about the students and the subjects as possible and by encouraging them to be open, honest, positive, but also constructively critical about their observations. Insights arising from peer observation are likely to be quite different from the kind of feedback you get from your students (Orsmond 1993). Comparing both sources of feedback can help you to build a comprehensive and multi-level picture of your teaching and suggest useful ideas for your teaching in the future.

1.10 Keeping a teaching diary

- Teaching diaries capture real time reflections that benefit longer-term teaching habits and orientations.
- Teaching diaries can be used to monitor, compare and analyse teaching experiences in ways that support a scholarly, reflective approach to teaching.
- Teaching diaries can ultimately save time and energy by capturing key recurring dynamics and patterns in particular classroom settings.

Keeping a teaching diary is a very valuable activity whether you will be teaching the same programme for some years to come, or you are required to hand over to someone else and mentor their teaching in the future. A teaching diary that records questions, problems, ideas, challenges and struggles that you and your students have encountered can represent an enormously useful professional development tool, and can provide raw material for refreshing, enhancing or even redesigning aspects of your programme with a view to continuous improvement and ongoing development of your teaching (Richards 1990; Brock et al. 1991).

You can record any kind of information or observation in the process of your teaching – pragmatic (e.g., 'not enough copies of a particular reading in the library', 'only a small number of students regularly accessed on-line discussion boards'); cognitive (e.g., 'students really struggled to understand X Y and Z, but very quickly grasped A, B and C, as evidenced by in-class assessments or quizzes'); emotional (e.g., 'there was a difficult conversation around socio-economic backgrounds when students were asked to read and discuss case study F'); collaborative (e.g., 'students really started to accelerate and improve their work after week 5 which was when a collaborative small group task was set').

These kinds of experiences and observations tend to be quite readily noticed by teachers if they are asked to watch and listen carefully for evidence of student engagement and learning. However, it is easier to notice such dynamics within your learner groups, but relatively difficult to recall the exact nature of these interesting and useful phenomena a year later – which is when such information could be extremely useful.

Short-term adaptations of your teaching and responses to student experiences are one thing, but longer-term improvements can really benefit from the keeping of a teaching diary. It is a practical tool that can help you to track and monitor and enhance your own performance and make the most of your teaching insights. Of course you will find that each student group is likely to be different, but it is generally true to say that teaching diaries equip teachers with information that might otherwise evaporate and have them feeling that they're somehow re-inventing their own wheel.

1.11 Having an academic mentor

- Trusted academic mentors are likely to have a positive impact on your career development.
- Selecting and securing an objective, supportive mentor is an important professional choice.
- You may need different mentors at key stages in your career or for different dimensions of academic activity.

While we have presented the specific teaching performance related guidance that can be derived from peer observation (in section 1.9), this section focuses on a more contextualized kind of guidance that can be achieved by harnessing the energies of an academic mentor. There are many shortcuts, tips, ideas, insights, strategies, problems and solutions in academic life that other people have encountered before you. You don't have to be on a lone and solitary journey, and you don't have to face or discover all of these things completely on your own. Well delivered advice at crucial points in your academic career can be invaluable. At the very least it can save you time. Sometimes it can have transformative effects.

While we have recognized that academia is often individualistic and competitive, we also know that those people who have found trusted mentors somewhere within their system experience benefits and achieve breakthroughs that would otherwise have been a lot more difficult. Indeed there is much evidence, across many organizational settings that mentors are good for your professional well-being (e.g., de Janasz et al. 2003).

Good mentors can enhance your career, can accelerate your journey to proficiency and can make you feel psychologically safer and more guided in the thorny terrain that university and college teaching sometimes presents. But finding a mentor is not always easy. There are good and bad mentors in any context. You need to be aware at least in some vague way about what you need at your stage of development, for different aspects of your working life. Some people who take on mentoring roles don't automatically have a positive impact on the lives and work of their mentorees. And in some cases the impact can even be damaging or destructive. However, a good mentor is a potentially powerful ally and you can reap the benefits of the relationship right throughout your life. We recommend that you spend some time looking for and securing positive healthy mentor relationships as you embark on and continue your teaching career.

Your choice of mentor will inevitably depend on your own preferences, likes, dislikes and priorities. There will be an element of serendipity and luck about finding a great mentor at crucial times in your career, but it helps to know what you're looking for. The literature on effective mentoring suggests that your mentoring relationship should be trust-based and power-free (Rymer 2002); multi-source and multi-level (Ensher et al. 2002); and monitored, nourished and adapted over time (Vincent and Seymour 1994).

Also, while one mentor is useful and professionally helpful, several well chosen mentors can be an even stronger asset. By having more than one mentor, you get to explore your ideas and plans through a range of different lenses and you have the advantage of seeing problems from a variety of perspectives. This is a useful way to become a reflective practitioner and a great route to a more considered, more comprehensive orientation towards your work as a teacher. Of course, it is likely that the kind of mentoring you need in the earlier stages of your life as a teacher is different from the kind of mentoring you may need when you're further on in your career, and key developments will help you to identify what kind of coaching will work best for you, when.

If mentors understand the range of different challenges that you will encounter they can help you to strike the right balance between teaching and other areas of your job, know when you're ready to move on to another phase or type of work and help you to ask and work on these kinds of tough questions, then you will find that they provide an invaluable service to you. Good mentors represent the epitome of what can be so empowering and positive about academic environments – they provide the collegiality, the critical support, the insight and the advice that people thrive on when they become academics and teachers in further and higher education.

1.12 Building your sense of entitlement as a teacher and scholar

- You are in the process of becoming an expert in your area.
- Your views and opinions about your topic are likely to be very useful for students whose perspectives are still probably very new compared to yours.
- You have a right to teach without having to know everything about your subject or knowing all possible answers that your students might ask.

Teachers often struggle with their sense of entitlement (Berhanu 2006). They worry about whether they have a right to teach others in an area they are still struggling to understand and master. They can feel somewhat embarrassed and self-conscious standing up in front of a class or having others assume that they are an expert in their field. These kinds of feelings tend to be particularly common among new teachers and it can interfere with the conviction and commitment that they bring to their job.

Teachers who feel entitled to teach also feel confident and poised within a teaching environment. Teachers who don't, can become consumed with self-doubt – even fear – and gradually lose their nerve, something that students can also absorb, making for a sort of nervous, tentative, disengaged teaching and learning experience. They feel ambivalent about being the expert in the room and they worry about whether they have a right to be at the top of the class, directing, facilitating, designing and determining the direction, the content and the nature of their students' learning. Try to recognize that even if you are very new to teaching, you have something important and valuable to bring to your students. Your own struggles with the subject you teach will help students just as much as those areas in which you feel competent and in control.

1.13 Avoiding professional jealousy

- Excessive competition and comparison can erode the enjoyable aspects of academic life.
- Focusing on the pleasures of academia is a nourishing exercise, particularly after a career setback.
- Be assertive about your career progression rights, but don't let setbacks destroy your own internal motivation and enthusiasm for your work.

It can seem that at college or university, your professional impact is constantly being compared to that of other people. Promotions systems seem to try to differentiate between people based on narrower and narrower distinctions, and the role of teaching is often lamented as either missing or inadequately accounted for in the assessment of whether or not someone deserves tenure, promotion or other types of accolades and rewards.

Comparing yourself to your colleagues can become an obsessive and dissatisfying game that can take you away from the purpose and pleasure that academic life might otherwise nurture. The true joy in life as Shaw (1950) once observed lies in 'being used for a purpose you consider a mighty one, the being a force of nature, rather than a feverish, selfish clod of ailments and grievances complaining that the world will not devote itself to making you happy'.

Being competitive and wanting to achieve in ways that differentiate you from others is not outlawed, nor do we suggest it should be. It's just that competition can quickly become dysfunctional. The gymnastics of competitive comparison can become a sort of soul-less pursuit in its own right. It can take you away from the reasons you may have wanted to become an academic in the first place. It can cause you to spend more time than you should poring over your various achievements, lamenting your lack of career progression, tinkering idly with your CV and having rather fractious discussions with the people who you think may have some influence over your next career move.

All of these types of activities may form part of your life as a teacher in college or university, but when they become the driving pursuit or the main direction for your energy they are likely to have damaging and personally undermining effects. If you find yourself spending a lot of time wondering what someone else did to deserve the promotion or the accolade that you failed to get, then maybe it's time to re-orientate yourself or to find a way of refreshing your commitment to your subject, your interest, your enthusiasm, your own unique, irreplaceable, unmeasureable (albeit inconsistently rewarded) talent.

1.14 Recognizing the power that comes with teaching

- Examine power relationships between students and teachers – where possible relating this to the subject matter that you teach.
- Create democratic classroom climates to enhance student engagement and to teach in more ethically aware ways.

Even if you are a passionate, enthusiastic and committed teacher, your influence on learners may not always be positive and empowering. Teachers have a lot of power in university settings. Their views, their voices and what they value has a currency that many students are prepared to accept without question (Beach 1997). When students sign up to the unequal power relationship that prevails between them and their teachers, several things happen.

First, they may be more likely to accept (or at least not to challenge) behaviour from teachers that they would not accept in other contexts. Second, they may unwittingly reinforce teaching behaviours, habits and patterns that don't support their learning. And third, they may not draw learning related problems to the attention of their teachers. Compliant, accepting, respectful students may contribute to a situation in which your teaching styles and actions are not subjected to enough criticism or evaluation. And while you may feel comfortable and get used to not being challenged or questioned, this may not be in the best interests of your development as a teacher or indeed the learning of your students.

Supplement the feedback you get from students with peer evaluations (see section 1.9). Work to create more democratic classroom environments by involving students in decisions related to the teaching of your subject. You will still have to call a lot of the shots, and some of the shots are already decided on by the design of the curriculum, but there is often more leeway than our habits and tendencies suggest.

We know that undeclared power in the classroom has very strong effects on behaviour and learning (hooks 1994) and we also know that the more democratic the classroom environment, the more of an active and empowered part students are likely to play in their learning (Brookfield and Preskill 1999). There is value in recognizing that by virtue of our position and knowledge, we do possess power that impacts on learner experiences. Explore the power and have your students do the same. Be aware of and critique it. Discover and discuss the principles upon which it is based (e.g., is your power based on your authority to grade and assess student performance; is it based on your expertise or your reputation?) If one of the fundamental aims of university education is to help to create critical thinkers, then a critical treatment of the power dynamics within the classroom is arguably an interesting interrogation to engage in.

Talking about power is a potentially fruitful conversation to have in any disciplinary setting. And in recognizing and discussing these power relations, both you and your students might be in a better position to distribute that power more evenly, helping learners to become vocal, critical, engaged and challenging about the subjects that you teach. It might all feel like a lot of hard work, but actually many people report that this takes some of the pressure and focus off them as teachers and creates all sorts of new levels of engagement among learner groups. This is an orientation that can transform a didactic and authoritarian approach to teaching, and set the scene for more interesting and satisfying experiences from everyone's point of view.

1.15 Revelling in the clandestine

- Don't underestimate the value of collegiate, trust-based learning climates.
- Differentiate between the student as 'customer' and the student as 'citizen'. Decide which model you prefer.
- Remember that some of the most powerful and effective moments of student learning cannot always be predicted, designed or measured.

> The official university places its trust in abstract and general systems that may have no purchase on truth or reality but that obey a transparent, if tyrannical, logic . . . The clandestine university, by contrast, places its trust in human beings working together, engaged in argument and dialogue.
>
> (Docherty 2005: 223)

This quote comes from an insightful critique of some of the ailments associated with higher education policy and practice. One of Docherty's most powerful arguments lies in his assertion that quality control systems within college and university environments tend to sustain the freedom of the consumer (which he defines as slavery) rather than the freedom of the citizen (which he defines as emancipation).

Furthermore, he argues that it is often the unstructured, unscheduled, unplanned and unmeasurable dynamics of teaching and learning that yield the most memorable and transformative results. It's easy to measure student attendance, grades, retention rates, performance averages and other quality-related gauges – but at best these can only be vague proxies of what's really happening in an educational environment. Revelling in the clandestine requires having a healthy scepticism for the measures that are applied to quality at college and university.

If we become too obsessed with the inevitably inadequate measures that are applied to the control and management of our universities, we might risk forgetting the principles of engagement, excitement and delight that committed educators bring to active learning environments.

1.16 Knowing your mystery ingredient

- Become aware of your strengths and your unique characteristics as a teacher.
- Remember that you don't have to be perfect in every aspect of teaching to be an outstanding teacher, nor should you always feel your teaching has to fit a standardized template.

Even after analysing thousands and thousands of student perspectives on excellent teaching, there still seems to be support for the idea that really excellent teachers possess a 'mystery ingredient' that could be most closely described as 'presence'. Brady and Bedient (2003) define presence as 'an ability to listen, to adapt, and to make effective choices in language and in emotions to help motivate students toward success'. But different teachers clearly exercise this ability in different ways. Our own analysis of teaching effectiveness data shows that many ratings of overall effectiveness are significantly higher than the more specific and common indicators of effective teaching such as organization, preparation, communication skills, knowledge, enthusiasm, ability to explain difficult material and so on. In other words, some teachers can score quite badly on things like preparation and even communication, and still in overall terms be defined by their students as outstanding teachers.

Your mystery ingredient is unique and may be what differentiates your particular kind of teaching impact among your students. It might be difficult to identify, measure or pin down. In your eagerness to engage in professional development as a teacher in higher education, take care not to 'overhomogenize' yourself in response to standardized recommendations of delivery, and take care not to rob yourself of your original and distinctive voice and style.

2

Focusing on key teaching skills and competencies

*Introduction • Developing the curriculum • Pre-lecture preparations
• Knowing the ingredients of effective delivery • Putting effective delivery
into practice • Post-teaching winding down • Encouraging interaction
• Preparing notes, study supplements and class documents • Integrating
academic writing into your life as a teacher • Staying up to date with your
material • Knowing the most important sources of information in your field
• Being part of a network of scholars • Being rigorous about the material
you teach • Developing supervision skills*

Introduction

Despite many new developments and changes in teaching and learning environments, there is a range of established skills and competencies that remain
relevant in most college and university settings. For this reason, Chapter 2
presents ideas about the basic skills associated with preparing and delivering
good teaching and learning experiences.

We will take you through some of the ideas, questions and actions
associated with developing and designing your curriculum and we present
some useful orientations towards planning, delivering and reflecting on your
lectures and other teaching sessions. We recognize that in addition to the

technical and intellectual tasks associated with teaching, there are also peaks and troughs in energy levels: the need to gear yourself up before key teaching sessions, to stay relaxed and focused during your teaching and to wind down afterwards. Such varying energy levels and related actions are the often unspoken rhythm associated with key teaching activities, and we give them some explicit attention in this part of the book.

We also explore some other practical basics like staying up to date with material, integrating writing into your life and ensuring that your supervision skills are sound. Overall then, this part of the book is particularly useful when you are planning and/or in the process of delivering a module for the first time, or making significant changes to a course you have already taught.

2.1 Developing the curriculum

- Many teachers find curriculum design and development an ambiguous and poorly defined activity.
- It's useful to start by thinking about broad learning objectives and course aims as a springboard for more detailed decisions about course content.
- Observing students, liaising with colleagues, interrogating existing curricula, course outlines and objectives are useful things to do when planning to design or develop the curriculum or aspects of it within your field.
- Remember that curriculum development is a creative process and think about ways in which your programme design can light fires of curiosity among learners in your discipline.

Issues surrounding the course curriculum tend to be a significant focus of effort, particularly for newly appointed teachers. You may be asked to take over responsibility for changing a pre-existing curriculum or to develop a new one from scratch. Teachers are often implicitly required to update or alter curricula, often on quite a regular basis, mainly in order to accommodate advances in the subject area, and sometimes in order to respond to changes in overall course/ programme requirements. When new teachers are faced with these kinds of common requirements and their related tasks, they often report feeling daunted. Many of them experience curriculum development as a difficult, ambiguous and poorly defined process (Hall et al. 1996).

To start with, tackling curriculum development or design is most fruitfully achieved by adopting quite a simple, holistic orientation. Before considering the detailed specifics of every part of the planned course or module, it is usually beneficial to reflect on your ideas about the overall aims of a programme or course of study, and what might be the best ways to achieve those broad aims.

Posing simple questions is a good way to initiate the generation of creative and appropriate ideas about curriculum design and development. What should all students know, be able to do, understand and have achieved by the time they have finished this course? You will need to consider curriculum aims, intended learning outcomes and content, but also issues relating to modes of course delivery, student support and assessment or examination processes.

In some instances specific pre-defined constraints must also be accommodated (e.g., specific learning outcomes may be dictated by outside professional bodies if they accredit your course. This can be true, for example, in the context of many engineering and healthcare professional programmes, but may also be the case for programmes in many other disciplines too).

Careful consideration of the design and appropriateness of course aims and intended learning outcomes is a critical first step. Once these are refined it is important to ensure that the content of the curriculum is designed to meet the overall aims and all the individual learning outcomes. Also, as you develop the detailed individual curriculum topics, additional appropriate learning outcomes may become apparent, allowing the document to further evolve.

Curriculum development can be a creative process if you allow yourself to treat it as its own form of discovery, and to learn from the processes in which you engage to achieve it. It should not simply be seen as a bureaucratic exercise, but rather as a way to bring alive and structure the teaching of your subject in a way that makes sense, that recognizes the key differences between basic and more advanced skills and knowledge in your area, and that considers the importance of pace and the gradual development of competence.

These are ideas that you, as an emerging expert in your subject, should work on clarifying for yourself, in collaboration with your colleagues and your students throughout your professional life. By observing and learning from your students' challenges, you will learn to differentiate between the parts of your discipline they readily master and the other areas that they more frequently struggle with. By consulting existing curricula in your subject and in other areas you may familiarize yourself with aspects of your subject that are generally seen as introductory, intermediate or advanced. By liaising with both experienced and new colleagues, you will be likely to absorb a more fine grained idea of how the challenges of your discipline and its related topics can be incorporated meaningfully and appropriately into a well designed, well paced, and well structured curriculum.

Remember also that it is likely that you will be able to tap into several sources of assistance when designing and developing a course. General principles of syllabus design and development are widely considered in the educational literature and college/university teaching centres usually routinely provide courses for staff that include elements of syllabus design. Exact detail of individual syllabus topics often follow in part or in full the content of relevant published textbooks. Content can also be guided by identification of suitable review-type articles published in discipline-specific journals and indeed by reviewing curriculum details of similar courses provided elsewhere.

Modification/update of a syllabus can additionally benefit from feedback obtained from past students as well as a detailed course log or commentary maintained by the lecturer (see also section 1.10).

It is important to present course aims, learning outcomes and the syllabus description in clear and unambiguous language. Learning outcomes in particular need to be carefully constructed and presented and it is best to avoid using generalized statements such as 'the student will gain an overall appreciation of . . .' The more unambiguous the document the more useful it will be, both for yourself and your students. Most institutions will have a standard template document used in the context of course description but it is often beneficial to prepare a more detailed version for presentation to the students themselves.

Many newly appointed teachers tend to be overambitious in terms of the breadth of topics they believe they can cover in a course (O'Neill et al. 2005). Ironically this is often particularly characteristic of the more enthusiastic and dedicated teachers. Gaining advice and feedback on draft syllabus details from more experienced colleagues, as well as comparison of the proposed syllabus with other course syllabi can help you to avoid this until you have built up sufficient experience yourself. It's probably a good idea to be cautious and circumspect as you plan to develop the curriculum, but also not to be too timid about building in exciting developments or experiences that will help to bring your discipline to life and that will appeal to your students' curiosity and engagement. There is an ancient saying that education is not so much the filling of a bucket as the lighting of a fire. Try to ensure that the potential for ignition is embedded in the courses and programmes that you play a part in designing.

Also remember that the territory is not the map. When you design a course and write a curriculum you are really only creating a signposting system that will guide either you or another teacher. How that topic is engaged with and how the material is delivered and received still very much depends on the talents and motivations of the teachers who do the teaching. No matter how well a curriculum is conceived, planned and designed, teachers and students need to engage actively with the curriculum and feel empowered to continue to develop and improve it based on their own experiences within the classroom and beyond.

2.2 Pre-lecture preparations

- Lectures are still a very common arena in which formal teaching and learning experiences occur, even in very up to date higher and further educational environments.

- A useful way to get ready to give a lecture or series of lectures is to prepare a detailed course information pack. Generating individual lecture plans with details of time frames, material to be covered and key activities is also a very useful mechanism for setting a solid foundation for effective teaching within formal lecture/tutorial times.
- Preparation time needs to be adequate. Don't underestimate how time consuming it can be, but look out for helpful shortcuts.
- Be familiar with locations, spaces, equipment and other physical conditions and constraints when preparing to deliver lectures.

For most on-campus programmes, the lecture remains one of the dominant 'tools' used to deliver the curriculum to students. Despite their well documented constraints and limitations, lectures still tend to form a strong backbone to a programme and to the learning experiences of students. In combination with other learning experiences, a good lecture can inspire, inform, engage, incite curiosity and encourage inquiry. A bad lecture on the other hand runs the risk of boring, disengaging, confusing, bamboozling and disconcerting students (and teachers). Some basic issues relating to good preparation and planning can help ensure that your lectures are characterized by all of the positive potential that they contain, and avoid some of the pitfalls which even the best teachers sometimes encounter.

Before planning individual lectures it is useful to decide on the general 'ethos' of the experiences you want to provide and facilitate for your students. You need to think about the underlying principles associated with the subject you are teaching, considering such questions as: what level of interactivity is appropriate? What should the balance be between presenting/explaining information, and other experiences that can reasonably be integrated into a lecture type format (illustrations, problems, case studies, learning insights and small group discussions)?

Think about how much information should be provided or signposted, and what kinds of information resources need to be secured for student access outside of the classroom. In terms of practical preparations, we have observed that teachers find it useful and grounding to prepare a concrete or on-line student course information pack for provision to all students before course commencement or during the first lecture. It is reassuring for students (and for you) if you use the first lecture to review the information provided in the course pack, set any ground rules and answer any initial questions the students may have.

Details of what is included in such course pack can vary, but can include: module description (aims, learning outcomes and syllabus details); methods/mechanics of delivery (via lectures, coursework, tutorials, etc.); reading material lists; criteria on which assessment will be based and the relative weighting allocated to each assessment instrument; a sample illustrative exam question with an associated marking template; a previous exam paper; a statement on lecturer expectations and general ground rules; contact details; and availability of lecturer outside of formal lecture slots. (See section 2.7 in this chapter for more detail.)

More fine grained lecture plans are also worthwhile developing. For each lecture, it is useful to sketch out the different subparts, key moments, information and activities that you plan to incorporate into the session. If your lecture is 50 minutes, then you will need to schedule and apportion time within that frame to the different essential themes that you want to cover, to activities or discussions in which you want your students to engage and to other experiences that you want to incorporate. Timing and pacing needs to be planned. Particularly if your class is large, even handing out materials or re-organizing the room set-up to facilitate small group discussions can eat into the time available. Lesson/lecture planning can provide an antidote to what might otherwise make you feel chaotic, disorganized or somewhat out of control. It is also a good way of ensuring that your students' attention and involvement remains as high as possible.

Most teachers will tell you that despite the inevitable benefits of talent, intelligence, expertise and experience, there is no substitute for adequate preparation for teaching. It is a confidence inspiring key to successful delivery. And while your preparations are underway it is important to keep overall module aims and individual learning outcomes clearly in mind when preparing each lecture. The provision of sufficient time to research and prepare each lecture is generally an important consideration. Hurried preparation is often an unavoidable reality for first time teachers.

Remember that in reality it can take anything from several hours to several days to plan, research, prepare and review each individual lecture. Few things in life are as stressful as sitting up in the small hours the night before your class in order to complete a lecture or wrestling with an uncooperative photocopier with only minutes to spare before a lecture is due to begin. Be realistic about the amount of preparation time you will need to feel well equipped to deliver your lecture – especially if this is the first time you'll be teaching it. But also exploit any helpful shortcuts that can lighten the load. Many textbooks now also have associated lecturer resource pages which can include copies of diagrams and handouts with reproduction permission for teaching purposes that you can distribute to your students. Such resources can be invaluable, particularly when time is short and demands on that time are high.

For newly appointed lecturers in particular it is desirable to begin preparing a lecture series several weeks before the course begins. Unless you are supremely confident about the material, make out additional lecture notes/memory aids to which you can refer during the lecture. You should not feel you have to be surreptitious when referring to such notes or aids. It is perfectly okay to consult additional documents periodically during any lecture and to make them available to students or direct them to where such details can be sourced.

The better prepared you are the more confident your delivery is likely to be.

It can be helpful for novice teachers in particular to do a dry run of a few lectures in order to boost confidence and get the timing right. On a more pragmatic level, it is also important to become familiar with the lecture hall layout and operation of the equipment before starting to teach in a new or unfamilar space. It is important to make adequate time available immediately before lecture delivery in order to review lecture overheads and to get yourself focused and mentally prepared for your lecture.

2.3 Knowing the ingredients of effective delivery

- The ingredients of effective delivery are easy to understand but often difficult to put into practice.
- As long as there are opportunities for interactivity and activity inside and outside of class, didactic (face-to-face delivery of learning material) teaching episodes can still be a useful and effective way to help students learn.
- Linking teaching sessions together can be achieved by invoking the last session at the beginning of the class and talking briefly about what's coming next at the end.
- Keeping in mind diverse learning styles and varying attention levels can help guide your efforts to vary your own style and keep your students engaged.

One of the most critical attributes of a good teacher is an ability to communicate information effectively in the classroom (see also section 1.1). 'Natural' teachers usually possess this talent inherently but it is something that also can be acquired. The principles of clear communication are well researched (see, for example, Chickering and Gamson 1987). The difficulty, however, for many of us is not one of understanding these principles but of consistently putting them into practice.

The basic tenets of clear communication are often quite self-evident. They include: defining your communication objectives at the outset; planning, researching, drafting, evaluating and revising the ideas and concepts you want to communicate; and always attempting to have a reasonably clear idea of the needs, assumptions, backgrounds and experiences of the people with whom you are communicating. However, making these principles play themselves out in your own teaching may be much more difficult than their apparent simplicity might suggest.

The value of the didactic

Lectures and other face-to-face formal learning sessions can still play an important part in the educational experience of further and higher educational students. Good didactic delivery, when combined with opportunities for interaction and active engagement, can still be a vital anchor with which to build competence and knowledge in almost any area. But it is also important to steer away from an uninspiring, monotonous transfer of information. Formal teaching sessions achieve their aims of engagement and learning by using a range of different techniques. Telling a story, posing a problem, asking a question, presenting a conundrum or a paradox, demonstrating the practical implications of a concept or illustrating your points in colourful imaginitive ways can all serve to ignite your students' levels of engagement and enhance their learning. And you can do these things without compromising the effective display of a logical train of thought, while also ensuring that you cover all the objectives associated with a specific teaching session.

Pacing, linking and contextualizing

At the beginning of each lecture it is useful to set the scene by briefly summarizing what was covered in the last lecture (e.g., 'Last week we looked at X . . . concluded that Y, and asked this puzzling question which focused on Z'). Then it is good to focus students on what's coming next (e.g., 'This week let's try to see if we can come up with a variety of answers to that question by . . .') It can also be worthwhile listing the main points/concepts to show how the content and focus of the class relate to the overall course objectives and intended learning outcomes. Likewise, at the very end of the lecture it is useful to summarize what was covered during that class period. If you are going to give students a vital instruction or piece of information at the very end of the class, remember that as the session draws to a close, students, even the most attentive ones are going to start thinking about their next class, focus on gathering up their bags and start switching on their mobile phones. Keep this in mind when wrapping up. It's worth thinking more explicitly about the attention levels and dynamics of your students during class delivery.

Attention levels during class

Students (just like anyone else) can maintain uninterrupted, high quality concentration only for a limited amount of time (Tileston 2005). Some research suggests that this time is unlikely to last for more than 10 or 15 minutes. Others suggest it might be considerably less than this, depending on a whole range of factors. What we do know is that because of limited and varying capacity for focused attention, it is a good idea to punctuate presenting information with other kinds of learning opportunities and activities, in order to revive, maintain or refocus both concentration and interest. You can also be sure that, at any given instant during the lecture, some of your students will at least transiently lose concentration. Periodic, brief revision of important 'information bites' imparted therefore is important in providing a second opportunity for the students to grasp a point or concept, and therefore continue to follow lecture progression.

Fifty minute lectures can only cover a limited number of points, concepts, skills, ideas or activities. It is counterproductive to attempt to cram too much into any one learning session. In addition, different students listen, read, absorb and think differently. You can't cater for all differences at every moment, but you can try to engage as many students as possible by varying your style and pacing, and ensuring the clarity of any of the material you present and distribute. The lecture structure should be evident throughout and it is helpful to signal clearly to students when you are moving on to consider a new point or concept.

So, any class is likely to contain a heterogeneous mixture of individuals displaying different levels of background knowledge, learning styles, levels of commitment, interest, motivation and ability. This situation is further complicated if the class consists of multiple cohorts of students undertaking different programmes. For some learners, your course may be of core interest and relevance in the context of their overall programme of studies, while for others it may be a more peripheral subject. In addition, student cohorts undertaking different programmes will be likely to have different profiles of background knowledge and may have different levels of competence, as judged for example by minimum programme entry requirements.

If your experience incorporates such diversity, it is important to pitch your teaching at a level that all the students can reasonably be expected to follow and to provide reference to background source material that would benefit student subgroups that may have less background knowledge than the wider group on the points/topics under consideration.

2.4 Putting effective delivery into practice

- Know about your students' views on what they associate with good and bad lecturing – decide to engage in that dialogue with them.
- Be aware of the basics of good lecturing, but don't be afraid to take risks in the interest of enhancing your practice as a teacher and your students' learning.
- Watch your students carefully in class. Their body language can signal important strengths and weaknesses in your teaching, but always try to ask students about their experiences to check that you're not misinterpreting their in-class signals.

The previous section has outlined some important general ingredients of effective communication. Here we focus more practically on more specific approaches to putting these principles into practice. Student feedback gathered in our own research tends to describe a good lecturer as someone who provides: clear module aims and syllabus details; clear lecture overheads and notes; encourages participation; provides practical examples of concepts; delivers lectures authoritatively and at an appropriate pace; provides adequate time for note-taking; is enthusiastic, approachable and displays a sense of humour. The same students say that bad lectures are characterized by disorganized delivery; pacing that is too fast or too slow; and accompanied by material that is unclear, impossible to access or difficult to read. Even very good and committed teachers can sometimes be vulnerable to making some other classic mistakes: the pursuit of an overambitious syllabus; inaccurate assumptions about background knowledge level; monotone delivery; failure to engage with the class; being or seeming unapproachable, uninterested or detached. These may all be the negative (if accidental) levers that serve to switch learners off or to develop negative associations between them and the material.

Despite the guidelines and advice that we provide, it is important to recognise that there is no single right or wrong way to deliver a lecture. Don't be afraid of exploring and experimenting with different delivery options or taking risks. Start off with the basics. Remember that your perception of your delivery and the reality for the students can be quite different (Perry 1988). For many the concept of student feedback equates to gathering written or oral student responses to a series of questions post-lecture or when a course is finished (see Chapter 1 for more details). The most effective and useful feedback however can come by simply observing the students during each lecture. This provides real time feedback, enabling immediate and responsive modification of your delivery practice where it is necessary, or enhanced potential for good communication and rapport between you and your students.

If a proportion of the students have quizzical or confused looks then it makes sense to ask them if there is something they don't understand. If some of the students are leaning forward or squinting as they copy overhead notes it may be that they are having difficulty reading the overheads. This is something you can easily check for yourself by viewing the overheads from the back of the class. It pays too to observe the students as they take notes. If they are writing constantly or under obvious pressure then you need to reflect on your lecture pace or you should consider providing copies of some/all of the overheads to the students. If the students display disinterest or signs of fatigue it may be time to alter delivery for example by initiating student participation, illustrating the relevance of the material to them, providing an example or anecdote, or even giving them a short break. Remember also though, particularly in large classes, that signals from students can be ambiguous and misleading. Interested students may 'look' bored to you (and vice versa), happy students may seem anxious and so on. Always check your interpretations of what you think their body language is conveying.

In addition to such informal observation of student behaviour it is good practice simply to ask them directly if lecture pace, size of overhead writing, etc. is appropriate. You can also consider the more detailed and elaborate approaches to student feedback that we have presented in Chapter 1. Alternatively you can encourage them just to flag such issues if they arise. As well as improving the effectiveness of delivery, such actions send a message to your students, a message that tells them they are important to you and that you are paying attention to them just as you require them to pay attention to you.

2.5 Post-teaching winding down

- It's common to experience emotional highs and lows at the completion of a teaching session.
- Capturing key feelings and reactions in writing using a teaching diary is a potentially useful way to help process and make sense of these feelings.
- Remember that teaching is physically and psychologically demanding and try to schedule time for winding down and relaxing.

Sometimes you will find that at the end of a formal teaching session you'll feel a sense of achievement, contentment or even relief. Other times you'll finish your teaching with a sense of disappointment, frustration or despondence. It has been observed that when teaching goes well for you and your students, there are few experiences so professionally energizing and affirming. But when it goes badly, there is very little that can give rise to the same sense of dejection. Remember that all teachers – including the excellent and the experienced – are likely to experience both sets of emotions at different stages and in different teaching contexts. The important thing is to harness these feelings in a positive and constructive way. Embrace and savour the positive feelings – they are part of the instrinsic reward for a job well done. Harness the negative feelings to galvanize your resolve to learn from any mistakes and continuously improve your teaching.

It is useful to note your post-teaching reactions and instincts in a teaching diary (see also section 1.10). Make records immediately after your teaching session, while events are fresh in your mind. By recording both positive and negative aspects of the teaching experience you have just had, you are generating a valuable resource for ongoing reflective practice. It is also worthwhile recording any broader issues that could impinge upon the learning environment and academic performance. Ask yourself specific questions about aspects of your teaching or the learning context that you may be concerned about. Did your students seem tired or disengaged? Might this be because of the nature of the subject matter, the time of the semester or a generally demanding schedule? Are there any difficulties with the layout of the teaching space or equipment? Are there issues of fitness for purpose to be reported to the appropriate responsible office? Making notes of any urgent action items required before you meet the class again may be particularly important.

Many teachers underestimate how physically and psychologically demanding it is to teach for even the standard 50-minute session. Research suggests that there are special demands associated with teaching in both large and small groups (Salzberger-Wittenberg et al. 1983) and that to feel physically depleted after teaching is a common experience (Gold and Roth 1993). Teaching requires sometimes intensive preparation; it demands the maintenance of considerable concentration; it involves thinking on your feet and having to deal with the unexpected; it entails the expenditure of physical effort and energy. All of this can give rise to a feeling of exhaustion once your teaching is over for the day. Teaching takes a physiological and indeed physical toll. Make sure you try to build in time to wind down, reflect, relax and rest once you have completed an intense period of teaching. Regular winding down, physical exercise and short breaks from work can create a much healthier orientation towards teaching both for you and for your students.

2.6 Encouraging interaction

- Studies show that in lectures/tutorials where students are given structured opportunities to interact with you and each other about a topic, they become more engaged, more empowered and more responsible, self-directed learners.
- When planning your teaching, devise interactive activities using discussion prompts, key questions or small group discussion activities.
- There is an extensive literature on the discursive and pedagogical benefits of student interaction in class. To find out more, Stephen Brookfield's book cited in this section is a good place to start.

Education and learning should never by characterized exclusively by simple and unidirectional transmission of facts, figures and concepts (Anderson et al. 1996). A balance of information flow that also incorporates active interaction among your students provides a context that is far more conducive to meaningful learning. Active interaction helps to engage student interest and concentration, and provides a degree of student ownership which can help deepen their commitment to the course. Student participation, particularly when prompted by good quality, evocative questioning, can underpin additional valuable and more general learning outcomes such as the development of logical reasoning (Johnson 1981), information synthesis (Samuelowicz and Bain 2001), deep learning (Grave et al. 1996), creative speculation, problem solving (King 1990) and capacity for rational debate (Mitchell and Sackney 2000). It also provides the lecturer with valuable feedback on the progress and level of understanding achieved by the students, can challenge and stimulate teachers themselves and provides a brief respite during lecture delivery.

Setting up a framework for such interaction can be achieved by various means. The lecturer for example may simply pose a question to the class and invite a response. The discussion can then be broadened by posing follow-on questions or by asking other students to comment upon or evaluate the initial response. Such an approach may be adopted at the level of an individual student or in a more collective manner by, first, organizing students into small groups or teams. The exercise may be confined to a single lecture or can be expanded by asking the students (as individuals or as groups) perhaps to research a question, concept or theory outside of class time and present/debate their findings during a future lecture.

The encouragement of meaningful student interaction requires adequate pre-planning by the teacher, as well as commitment from their students. The role of the lecturer is largely to devise and provide an appropriate framework for the interaction, initiate the interaction, and act as devil's advocate and facilitator of interaction among students.

To be successful this should be achieved in an encouraging and non-threatening environment and the interaction must be *meaningful*. Think about the questions you typically ask your students or perhaps the ones you would like to ask. Keep in mind that if you ask superficial, multiple choice, or yes/no kinds of questions, you may test basic recollection or put your students' guesswork to the test, but likewise, you risk only eliciting superficial engagement and responses from your students (Ramsden 2003). Interaction will be far more successful if probing but answerable questions are posed. Try an approach that gradually escalates student engagement: ask an initial, relatively easy, question to build confidence and to set the scene for interaction. Then follow up with gradually more challenging problems, questions or issues that build on the earlier responses. The initial question provides an opportunity to all the students (and not only the brighter ones) to contribute. This draws the students into further interaction. The subsequent interaction then helps to drive and support deeper learning (King 2000). In addition to initiating the process, you will probably find that you need to facilitate the interaction further by providing hints or additional pieces of information if the process begins to stall, or perhaps to guide the discussion in a particular direction.

As well as devising and researching appropriate questions/topics to drive interaction, it's important to do other things to create a class ethos and atmosphere conducive to meaningful student interaction. In order to partici-pate students must have confidence in the process and not feel threatened by it. This can be achieved in a number of ways. If the class is initially quiet/unresponsive it may take an element of 'cajoling' on your behalf to get things started and to establish trust. The interaction should always be driven in a supportive and positive atmosphere. Responding to student contributions should not be (or seem) sarcastic or designed to embarrass. Much more bene-ficial is a constructive analysis of the contribution, encouraging students to think through their answers and get closer to achieving their own insights while carefully and supportively exploring any flaws in logic, inaccuracies or points of disagreement in their arguments.

It can be counterproductive to pose a question to an individual student without some indication that he/she can provide a reasonable contribution. By inviting contributions generally from the class (or a specific subgroup, such as the second row) the process is not as threatening to any individual student. While all the class will benefit from observing interaction, individual students will benefit most from active participation in the process. If the contributions are constantly being provided by a small number of specific students inter-action can be broadened by introducing the principle that once a student makes a contribution they are relieved for a time from further contribution to the particular topic under debate.

For some teachers and for some disciplines orchestrating regular and mean-ingful student interaction can be more challenging than for others. However, the overall educational benefits for the students are worth the effort. For a more comprehensive treatment of the theoretical underpinnings of the benefits of an interactive classroom environment, read *Discussion as a Way of Teaching*, Brookfield and Preskill (1999).

2.7 Preparing notes, study supplements and class documents

- As you plan your teaching, consider how much additional material you might want to include as part of a supplementary course pack for your students.
- Remember that too much additional material might blunt students' infor-mation gathering motivation and skills, whereas too little may leave them feeling abandoned and undirected.
- Course packs can contain a wide variety of material and depending on your subject might include websites, reading lists, photographs, newspaper reports as well as more conventional notes to back up lectures.

Lecture notes, study supplements and other learning-related documents, handouts and diagrams are additional learning supports that you may consider preparing for your students. If well integrated with other resources like textbooks and library or on-line reading, they can form an invaluable bedrock of signposts, references and explanations to assist and reassure your students. Clearly you need to be selective about this. Spoonfeeding with mountains of additional notes which have been assiduously and time consumingly prepared by you is probably unlikely to be an appropriate strategy, even if you teach particularly difficult or rapidly changing topics. In a world where gaining access to good sources of information is an important skill for your learners to develop, helping them to learn about the right places to look may be more useful to them than handing them that information on a plate. However, preparing limited quantities of well chosen student notes and supplements can add enormous value to the experiences of your students as well as to their sense of confidence and security as they learn to tackle and understand the topics that you teach them. It may be particularly useful when detailed explanations are necessary, if there is a unique feature in your course that is poorly dealt with or insufficiently explained in the literature, or at times when students lack the initial confidence or skills to look for useful and important sources of information related to the topics on your course. So being selective is important, but also being able to identify likely or common gaps in the resource bases to which your students have access is a good way to help to strike a balance between oversupplying them with information they could easily learn to find themselves and leaving them unsupported in important areas of your course.

Once you have made the decision about whether and how much additional information to provide, like your lectures themselves, these extra supplements may require regular review and updating in light of experience, modifications to the curriculum and advances in the subject matter. Incorporating consideration of notes provided during reflective practice and in student feedback requests allows you to optimize the evolution of your notes, increasing their usefulness to your students. As always, a decision on what to include in a book of notes or other supplementary material will require careful consideration of the lecture or lecture series' aims and intended learning outcomes, as well as practical considerations (e.g. the availability and quality of relevant supporting textbooks, papers, e-resources and other learning supports).

A book of notes can simply consist of copies of your lecture slides or text which provides supplementary lecture material. But it can also add colour, imagination and substance to your teaching by incorporating pictures, extracts, assessments, newspaper articles, problems, cases, experiments, research evidence, examples, images, questions, self-assessment quizzes or a combination of all of these. We have found that different teachers have different opinions about the relative advantages and disadvantages of providing this kind of supplementary material for their students. A lot of their reservations are based on the extra time commitment that the prospect of this kind of preparation entails. And of course you do need to be pragmatic about how much time you have to do this and whether this represents the best use of that limited resource.

However, we do know that if continually preoccupied by copying down information provided on your slides/overheads, students are robbed of the opportunity to digest, consider, evaluate or critically explore their understanding of the material you are teaching as well as of the opportunity to make their own contributions and ask their own questions as the lecture progresses. Errors made by the student during the transcribing process may introduce confusion and misinformation in their notes. While the ability to transcribe and summarize large volumes of material within a constrained time frame may indeed be a useful and pragmatic skill to acquire, it is rarely listed among the most important learning outcomes of any programme of study. Provision of well structured and well integrated notes and module resources does help to overcome the dilemma that teachers often face when considering how much time they need to spend transmitting information versus other important pedagogical activities in which students engage more actively. The preparation of these kinds of resources also allows you to teach at a faster pace (which can be particularly valuable if your time budget is tight and if you want gradually to encourage increasingly independent learning climates among your students).

However, keep in mind also that the free availability of, for example, exact copies of all your overheads can give rise to unintended outcomes such as reduced lecture attendance and student disengagement if they are not regularly making additional notes or partaking in interactive discussions. A useful balance is often struck by making a proportion of your overheads available in course notes. One approach is to make 'skeletal' copies of all the overheads available, with selected points of information omitted (this should be clearly flagged on the overheads). A variation of this entails the complete omission of some overheads, with the inclusion of those that contain particularly critical information, extensive data, complex diagrams or any other information difficult to transcribe in a timely and accurate manner. Again it is important to number overheads and clearly flag missing overheads, so that students can retrospectively and seamlessly link transcribed and provided information. This approach often balances the advantages and disadvantages of the alternative 'all or nothing' approaches.

As you have seen, course notes can contain much more than copies of overheads. Like any aspect of your teaching, your own creativity, imagination and commitment can lead you to developing supports that will amaze and delight your students. So be creative and adventurous, remembering that student notes can provide a blanket of reassurance and a strong foundation for student study strategies outside your classroom, but also recognize that spoonfeeding your students may exhaust you and may not in the end do them any real favours on their learning journey.

2.8 Integrating academic writing into your life as a teacher

- Many academics lack confidence and feel unsure about aspects of the academic writing process.
- Deliberate writing strategies are necessary to adopt if writing is to become an integrated and nourishing aspect of your professional life.
- Simple supports like writers' groups and writers' retreats can help you to adopt healthy effective orientations towards writing.
- Writing for publication is often challenging, and it is essential to accept that several revisions (both before and after submitting your paper) may be necessary before seeing your work in print.
- Effective, regular writing can boost your career and also enrich your teaching in a range of important ways.

If you are an academic, teaching is very unlikely to be your only responsibility. Most academics are under pressure to carry out a wide range of other duties that take up time and energy. More particularly – and often more problematically – they are required and expected to write and publish in their areas of expertise. More generally, writing skills are often seen as absolutely central to your competence as an academic in the realms of both teaching and research.

This is something that many members of faculty feel quite uncomfortable about. While there tends to be an assumption that all academics can write well, many of them don't (Boice and Jones 1984). To enjoy writing and to be motivated to write regularly, it has to be seen as something positive that feeds other aspects of professional life or that is worth doing simply for its own sake. Many academics have negative views about academic writing (Hjortshoj 2001). Furthermore, many of them lack confidence and strategies for integrating writing into their lives (Becker 1986; Zerubavel 1999).

In the light of this, it may be reassuring to know that there are strategies and orientations, some of them quite simple, that can be adopted that ensure that you develop and nurture your writing skills and that these skills continue to develop throughout your academic career. By adopting a deliberate academic writing strategy you will make a habit of engaging in important activities that will have a positive impact in the classroom and in the context of your own research and publishing plans (see, for example, Murray and Moore 2006).

Why writing is important

Apart from the pressures and expectations associated with academic writing, there are more positive ways to view the tasks and activities it requires. Writing in academia allows you to achieve a variety of goals. Through writing you can articulate important ideas in structured ways; generate and disseminate new knowledge; publish research; engage in considered commentaries; conduct reviews that contribute to your understanding of a topic as well as help others to learn more about it; produce pedagogical pieces that focus on approaches to teaching certain topics; and use your own writing skills and experiences to help students write effectively too. Writing allows you to focus on various facets of your expertise and it can be the manifestation of your competence, scholarship and hard work.

Writing can be personally very satisfying; it can help to keep you up to date with your subject area and relevant educational principles/concepts; it can be an enjoyable activity that energizes and enthuses you. All of this can make the pressures of writing easier to face, can help you develop your own academic profile and it can have positive downstream benefits to your own teaching. If you decide to integrate academic writing into your professional life, it can trigger a deeper level of reflective practice, again helping you to evolve your own teaching for the better. And if you pursue a writing strategy in particular ways it can also be beneficial in the context of driving your career progression. In these ways, writing may indeed be one of the fundamental activities of scholarship (see Elbow 2000).

Many experts in writing (e.g., Elbow and Belanoff 2000; Schneider 2003) assert that everyone can write. However, many academics don't feel as if they are natural writers and often express fear and anxiety when it comes to submitting their writing to the scrutiny of experts within their field (McGrail et al. 2006). Even when they have gained confidence and feel competent, it can still feel like an impossible task to write regularly and to good effect.

If these feelings (or even just some of them) apply to you, then it's probably comforting to know that your writing habits and skills can be dramatically improved simply by taking certain deliberate steps to build writing into your work schedule (Zerubavel 1999) and by engaging in writing supportive interventions. Some of these may be available within your own work context, but others you may have to initiate yourself. Two tried and trusted examples of activities and interventions that can kick start, enhance or develop your writing orientation are: writers' retreats (see for example, Grant and Knowles 2000; Moore 2003) and writers' groups (see Murray and Moore 2006). Writers' retreats involve groups of academics creating a temporary 'writing sanctuary' for anywhere between one and five days or so to focus, in a small community of practice, on specific writing tasks. During this intensive writing time participants provide help and assistance to one another, sometimes with the help of an expert facilitator. Writers' groups are similar, but easier to integrate into the normal weekly calendar where people meet regularly (say once a week) to discuss their writing projects, to share their successes and failures, and to benefit from the support and advice that might be difficult to find when working in isolation. There is no particular mystery about these interventions: they simply provide focused arenas in which you can address issues of competence and confidence in your writing. You may be fortunate to work in an environment that helps you to do this anyway, but many academics do not receive sustained support for their writing tasks, despite the pressure they feel to write and publish. These kinds of support become all the more relevant in situations where this pressure exists.

Other activities that can help you to write effectively and with more pleasure than might otherwise be the case include: reading publications aimed at helping individuals to write more effectively; attendance at writing enhancement programmes, courses or workshops; and examining critically the ways in which you use and manage time. In most academic environments it pays to view writing as an integral part of your teaching career.

The writing process is certainly time consuming. If you get used to planning and outlining your writing tasks, you can achieve a lot of progress by grabbing a few hours here and there from your routine schedule to pursue a writing project (Zerubavel 1999; Murray and Moore 2006). This can be as productive as setting aside longer blocks of time in which the writing project takes priority.

Like any project, a writing project requires adequate planning and commitment from beginning to end. To maximize chances of publication it is important not just to invest sufficient initial time and effort in order to identify and refine your publication idea, but also (and this is something that academics seem less likely to do), to choose and analyse your target journals with care (Murray 2005). A short list of potential journals is usually easily assembled on the basis of your own knowledge of your area, journal database searches and scanning the journal listings of well known publishers. A detailed review of the aims and scope of each journal as well as in-depth analysis of relevant articles already published in the journal usually allows you to identify the most suitable target journal for your work.

When writing for publication it is important not only to consider the publication criteria but also to have a knowledge of your target journal's 'instructions to authors' and to have these in mind while you are writing. When writing a manuscript it is usually important to highlight the core purpose/rationale of the paper, how it is different from previous papers and what its particular contribution is. It is usually also helpful to ask an experienced, trusted colleague to read and comment upon the paper before preparing a final draft. Some people find this very difficult to do, particularly in competitive academic environments. If you find the prospect of sharing your work a daunting one, then perhaps a writers' group or retreat would be of particular benefit to you.

Remember that when you submit a paper to an international peer-reviewed journal within your field, it can take up to six months to get feedback from the editor. It is often very common for submissions to be rejected, to be accompanied by hard-hitting comments or to require major revision. If the decision about your work falls into these categories, it is important not to become discouraged: revising and resubmitting work should be seen simply as part of the scholarly writing process. Besides, a paper revised in line with peer review is usually stronger and something you'll be more proud of in the end. If you resubmit the revised paper to the same journal make sure to submit a very clear and detailed letter of revision, which outlines the revisions and shows clearly and specifically how you have responded to reviewer comments.

More generally though, working to become a confident, regular writer can really help to build your confidence in many other ways too. Being a published writer endorses your scholarship, and understanding the rigours and challenges of writing for different audiences at different levels can help you to craft your expertise and mould it for different purposes. This is something that is likely to have a positive impact on your capacity to understand your subject more deeply and to teach its complexities and subtleties to your students.

2.9 Staying up to date with your material

- Keeping on top of developments in your subject area reinforces your confidence and competence as a teacher.
- Where feasible, align your teaching with your research.
- Get your students to research key developments and together learn more about emerging areas within your discipline.

Academic disciplines by their very nature, do not remain unchanged. They are the subject of continuous research, investigation, debate and reinterpretation. When writing a new course or taking over a pre-existing course it pays to ensure that teaching material, course outlines, key principles and lecture content are as up to date as possible. Some fields are particularly difficult to stay on top of: high-tech, scientific, engineering or computing disciplines, can see dramatic new changes and breakthroughs every few months.

Regularly updating your material, however, can be a genuine challenge, particularly if you are teaching higher level courses in fast moving areas. Meeting this challenge requires significant time and effort, which along with many of the activities we recommend, requires you to make a call about how much time you can afford to devote to keeping your teaching as up to date as possible. Most students can tell stories of teachers who use the same ragged overheads year after year. The advice in this section should at the very least help you consider the ways in which you can avoid fitting that particular well known stereotype.

As your career progresses it is likely that there will be even greater demands on your time. You wouldn't be the first teacher to succumb to the temptation to postpone updating your lecture material. But it might not be as daunting a prospect if you consider the following strategies:

1 Commit to evaluating significant new textbooks in your area. Complementary inspection copies are generally available on request from the publisher.
2 Undertake regular keyword literature searches in your area. In most instances limiting the search parameters to 'reviews' will reduce the number of hits identified to manageable levels and a review, by its nature, will provide a broad ranging update of the area.
3 Set student coursework tasks that will have an added benefit of updating you in fast moving areas. A student essay or project focusing upon a hot topic relevant to your course can automatically provide you with a bird's eye view of developments and a ready-made list of appropriate references – and this exercise has the added benefit of co-opting students in the active development of both your curriculum and their knowledge.
4 The time and cost it takes to attend a major conference in your field of expertise, perhaps on an annual basis, is an investment in your professional development. It will help you become more familiar and comfortable with key researchers in your area, give you first hand access to new ideas and provide new perspectives which can help update class material.
5 At a more strategic level, ask your head of department to assign a course to you which is closely related to your research interests (or offer to develop such a course). Aligning your teaching and research interests can have clear advantages for both activities and will maximize the efficient use of your time.

2.10 Knowing the most important sources of information in your field

- Don't underestimate the usefulness of basic sources of information including popular textbooks in your area, especially when teaching introductory courses.
- Utilize internet resources to enhance your knowledge of key sources but guard against time-consuming information overload.
- Informal collegiate links can be a rich source of useful information.

The last section focused on issues and activities that are worth considering when working to stay up to date with your material. One of the fundamental prerequisites for keeping up to date is to be able to identify the most important sources of information. Who are the most prolific writers/researchers in your field? What are the most important breakthroughs? What are the points of debate or division of opinion in your area? These questions are worth continuing to focus on as you develop as a teacher and an academic. Being able to answer them will help you to develop or update your course curriculum, to teach effectively and competently, to prepare student support material and to set appropriate coursework. Your experience and background will almost certainly mean that you have already had some practice in identifying the most important sources of information in your own field. But even those with extensive experience in a subject area are unlikely to have identified all sources of relevant information without regular, systematic and extensive searching for such sources.

Standard, basic information sources are usually a good starting point. Examples include student textbooks and journal literature relevant to your area. Publications from learned societies (see also section 2.11, 'Being part of a network of scholars') can often represent a particularly rich source of relevant educational material, as can discipline-focused education journals. Now that internet search facilities such as Google Scholar are freely available, you can usually narrow down your sources of information quite efficiently and without too much time or trouble. But be cautious about indiscriminate internet searching and always check the quality of the information you are sourcing by interrogating its review processes and origins.

A wide variety of additional information sources is also likely to be available to you, the exact profile of which will depend upon your own subject area. Conferences, summer schools or other focused gatherings of subject experts can often be a source of high-level information. Depending upon your discipline area sources such as governmental or other institutional records or publication stocks might also be important. If your teaching has an industrial/applied dimension the homepages or other publications of companies or industrial organizations can be useful too, providing product-related background and technical information. In some disciplines company annual reports are often worth scanning as they often contain data (e.g. market size and value) that is difficult to obtain elsewhere.

If your teaching has an applied dimension, the patent literature represents a rich, unique and often untapped source of teaching information. All patents contain a detailed background section, providing an extensive review of 'prior art' in the field, as well as a detailed technical description of the invention being patented. Patent databases (see, for example, www.uspto.gov) are easily searchable and full patents of interest can be purchased at a reasonable cost.

Additional sources of information that we often overlook may be right under our noses. They include research theses and tapping into the work and knowledge of our own colleagues. A research thesis will usually contain an introductory background section which provides a comprehensive and up to date overview of the topic under consideration. Trusted teaching and research colleagues might be happy to share relevant information and experience/knowledge or to suggest an information source that you may not have identified. If you have a college librarian, this is also someone who can be of great help, particularly in identifying sources of specific information you may be having difficulty in identifying yourself. Information overload can sometimes be more of a risk in preparing for teaching than a lack of information. Apart from wasting valuable time, you can find yourself feeling overwhelmed and confused by the sheer volume of information a comprehensive search can yield. When learning the most important sources of information in your field, you need to work on striking a balance between being exhaustive and being selective. You'll become intuitively better at doing this as you gain experience and confidence.

2.11 Being part of a network of scholars

- Good networks can be local, national or international.
- Networking takes effort and initiative, but is usually worth it.
- Joining scholarly societies and attending conferences are good routes to developing your networks.

As we have already noted, teaching can be quite a solitary activity. It can be easy to forget that you are also part of a wider family – those who have chosen teaching in academia as a profession. Networking with colleagues can be beneficial in many ways. It provides an opportunity to learn from them and share information. It sets up the potential for collaboration and can facilitate a social dimension within your professional circle. Being part of an academic family can give you support in many ways and can be a nourishing antidote to the sense of isolation that teachers can sometimes encounter, particularly at the beginning of their teaching career. You can establish excellent networks at different levels – local, national or international. This can involve interaction with just one individual or with groups of many scholars and teachers.

Local networking can often be particularly helpful for newly appointed teachers. While training initiatives and support measures are often available from centralized services provided by your institution, the most immediate and effective guidance is often available simply by seeking it out and chatting with experienced colleagues.

Networking activities can range from informal conversations over a morning coffee to more formalized arrangements, such as participation in a mentoring scheme (see section 1.11), writers' groups (Murray and Moore 2006) or peer networks. Whatever the approach, it can be very beneficial to engage with colleagues. They can provide you with advice/guidance on teaching-, learning- and examination-related issues as well as on university administrative procedures.

On a broader scale, joining national or international societies relevant to your discipline is usually well worth the effort and membership fee. Most societies publish a society journal with priority availability to members. Scholarly societies often publish more general scholarly journals available to members at reduced subscription rates. These journals can contain useful and informative education-related sections. In the initial phase of your career as a teacher, such education-focused articles can provide you with good ideas and strategies for developing your teaching. And, as you gain more experience these journals can provide a platform in which to publish papers of your own.

Societies also usually organize one or more conferences per year. We emphasize again that these conferences can provide you with a hugely valuable resource in terms of both discipline-specific education and research orientated presentations and provide a framework in which to network on a more individual level with other conference attendees. This kind of networking can form the basis of lasting cooperation in research and/or educational endeavours, as well as the development of lasting friendships and connections beyond the walls of your own institution.

Developing your network is a way of raising your awareness of emerging issues giving you perspective beyond your local context and enhancing your competence as a teacher and a scholar.

2.12 Being rigorous about the material you teach

- Rigour is a key characteristic of competent, well-planned, evidence-based teaching.
- Rigour provides you with the freedom to tell students you don't know something – and then commit to finding out the answer.
- A commitment to rigorous teaching is usually worth the effort in terms of enhancing your profile as a credible, conscientious teacher.

One of the most important characteristics of a good college or university teacher is the rigour with which they approach their topics and the extent to which they transmit that rigour to their students (Axtell 2000). A course syllabus is just a collection of words on a piece of paper. What brings the syllabus to life is how it is taught and this can have a profound effect upon student commitment and learning. At the core of excellence in teaching is rigour. In addition to its obvious impact upon the quality of student learning, it lies at the centre of academic integrity and professionalism. Your reputation as a teacher with both students and colleagues depends upon your ability to communicate and interact effectively with students and the rigour of your teaching. In addition, teaching well and rigorously provides you with a sense of worth and fulfilment as a teacher.

Being rigorous, like many other aspects of teaching, requires ongoing commitment, a heavy investment of time and energy, and spans all facets of your teaching. It demands adequate initial planning and research in terms of syllabus design, and ongoing modification. It demands adequate preparation of lectures, student notes and coursework. It demands adequate post-delivery reflective practice, feeding into continuous improvement of your teaching. It is particularly important in the context of design and execution of student assessment (see also sections in Chapter 6).

Bluffing or skimming over material will not deceive students for very long. In addition, students' own commitment to rigour will also often mirror the teacher's (Bean 2001). Rigour often manifests itself in 'going that extra mile' in terms of preparation and delivery. It is generally evident to students in terms of the command you display of your subject area, your preparedness and your ability to provide considered arguments, authoritative discussion or evidence, particularly if a teaching session goes in an unexpected direction. Rigour also relies on your follow-up (e.g., providing a comprehensive answer in a subsequent lecture to a question you could not immediately answer at the time it was posed).

Rigour is also characterized by an aspect less obvious to the students. For example, the fact that coursework assignments run smoothly is often testament to careful design or the fact that all elements of a syllabus are covered at an appropriate pace exactly within the allotted time frame usually conceals considerable lecturer planning and effort. The more rigorous you are the more effortless and professional your teaching will usually appear.

2.13 Developing supervision skills

- Supervision can be a particularly intense and demanding form of teaching.
- Setting clear goals and agreeing groundrules in the student/supervisor relationship can prevent subsequent difficulties or problems.
- It is important to strike a good balance between undersupervision where students feel abandoned, and oversupervision where students are not empowered to drive and manage their own project.

It has often been recognized that supervising student work is one of the most demanding, complex and sophisticated form of teaching that there is (see Brown and Atkins 1988). As part of their routine duties most teachers are required to supervise various student academic endeavours. At undergraduate level this can include supervision of mini-projects, laboratory practicals and final year research projects. Many teachers also supervise postgraduate students undertaking masters or doctoral programmes largely/exclusively by research. Supervision of postgraduate students is complex, high-level and extensive.

Effective supervision is difficult and demanding. Not only does it require intensive levels of engagement with individual students or small groups, the supervision process also calls on our skills in a way that requires us to customize our competencies in directing and supporting student work. Professional competence, accessibility, good interpersonal skills and a willingness to engage in supportive, critical dialogue are among the most important characteristics of an effective supervisor (e.g., McMichael 1993).

Professional competence and knowledge of the research topic area is essential to the initial assessment of the merits of a proposed research topic; providing appropriate technical guidance to the student; assessing and advising the student of the merit of the research work undertaken; and guiding the student in successfully publishing or otherwise disseminating the research results. Appropriate accessibility is required to allow for optimal student/supervisor interaction. Teachers undertaking active research in particular are invariably under constant time pressure. This can easily result in undersupervision, whereby contact with the student is reduced to a suboptimal level. It is best therefore to integrate regular formal, uninterrupted meetings with the student into your timetable, along with advising the student on your policy/ availability for additional unscheduled meetings or interaction. Effective communication with the student right from the beginning is also a major factor in providing successful supervision. This also relies on good interpersonal skills and the fostering of a close professional relationship with the student. From the very beginning of the supervisor relationship it is important to outline to the student what your expectations of them are and to understand their expectations of you and the process.

Supervisors normally expect students to drive and be responsible for their research activity in the context of an agreed programme of work; to plan, execute and evaluate individual work packages; to keep deadlines; to put effort into developing/enhancing appropriate written and oral technical communication skills; to maintain regular contact with the supervisor; and to behave in a generally professional manner.

One of the most difficult facets of supervision is to optimize the level and type of interaction you have with the student. For postgraduate students embarking on what effectively is the beginning of an independent research activity, it is often argued that supervisors should generally act as a facilitator, advisor, critic and guide as opposed to too closely directing what the student does. However, the level of direction may need to vary depending on the stage of the project and the confidence of the student (Woodhouse 2002). It seems to be good practice, for example, to allow a student to formulate a research plan and then critique the plan, as opposed to putting too much direct input into planning the research initially for the student. Through such feedback the student grows intellectually and learns from his/her initial errors and break-throughs. The student/supervisor relationship and the level of input needed will also of course change with time, with the student generally requiring more direct supervision during the initial phases of the work.

From time to time, difficulties can arise with regard to projects you are supervising and it is good to be prepared for such an eventuality. Many of these can be prevented if there are clear ground rules and expectations between student and supervisor. Students should have a good idea about how much contact time a supervisor will be able to give to helping them with their project. Setting a schedule of meetings at the beginning of the process can form the basis for a good working rhythm. Supervisors should be expected to help, read drafts and make suggestions for revision and enhancement, but students should also be aware that they need to drive and manage the project themselves. Difficulties can arise when ground rules like these are not established or not observed. Regular meetings, clear goals and feedback, and active engagement are all important dimensions of a good supervisor/student relationship as are providing support, suggestions and encouragement to a student when the project hits a difficult phase.

Furthermore it is good practice to keep a written record of your interactions with the student and input into the project along with student progress reports. Both student and supervisors should familiarize themselves with the instutitions relevant academic regulations, policies and procedures.

3

Focusing on your students

Introduction

Self-awareness and mastering basic principles and competencies are both important foundations on which to build effective teaching strategies, activities and reflections. These are issues that we have explored and developed in Chapters 1 and 2 of this book. Chapter 3 focuses on a range of strategies and activities that often distinguish teachers who are seen as having had an exceptional influence on their students' engagement, development and learning (Chickering and Gamson 1987).

In an academic world where many people and responsibilities are competing for your attention, it is often difficult to focus on the needs, requirements, difficulties, challenges and concerns of your students, even for a short time. Add to this the phenomenon of large classes and learners who may need particular kinds of help and support in responding to the challenges of your subject, and you can end up feeling overwhelmed by the needs of other people. We hope that the following cluster of reflections and ideas will help you to develop a strategy that allows you to focus in effective and efficient ways on your students. We believe that it is possible to create a learning environment in which they feel nurtured and cared about, and in which you can show your interest in them, without making unreasonable sacrifices in the context of your professional and personal life.

Partially, this can be achieved by setting down reasonable boundaries and clarifying your expectations of them as well as their expectations of you. Partially, it is about adopting more streamlined ways of helping students to learn. And partially it is about tapping into that part of yourself that does care about your students and is prepared to give time and energy to helping them to make the most of their experiences at college or university. In this part of the book then, we present some very basic practical ideas, from ways of helping you to remember your students' names to having consultation times that don't change from week to week. But we also tap into some established pedagogical and educational literature in order to explore some interesting principles such as learning breakthroughs, learning styles, multiple intelligences and learning communities in order to contribute to your repertoire of possible approaches to focusing in positive and informed ways on your students and their learning experiences.

3.1 Having office hours that everyone knows about

- Having regular, predictable office hours is a useful time management tool and is reassuring for your students.
- If you are permanently tied to your desk, at the mercy of your students' most trivial of queries, you are not doing yourself, or them, any favours.
- Commit to your office hours – clarify students' expectations about the times that you will be available exclusively to them, and then assert your right to devote other times of the day and week to other activities.
- Stay focused on your students during the office hours you have allocated to them – take the consultations seriously by eliminating normal distractions such as mobile phones, emails or other interruptions.

In many university and college settings, having regular office hours for consulting with your students is a requirement and it's something that you implicitly sign up to when you take on your role as a teacher. There are a few caveats associated with having office hours that might be useful to consider implementing in your own teaching setting.

If you ensure that your office hours are held at exactly the same time from week to week, if you work to make them an unchanging and predictable part of your weekly calendar, this can reduce rather than increase your workload, or at least contain student consultations in a way that is likely to be manageable. Stable, reliable office hours don't even have to be interminably long (not even if you teach very large groups) to provide a safety net for students and to make them feel confident that you are delivering on your side of the bargain in the teacher–learner relationship. It's worth trying to keep your office hours sacrosanct and really work to make yourself available during that time.

This has the effect of preventing students from coming at you from all sides at any time of the day or night. Without office hours that students know about, their queries, questions, concerns and uncertainties are more likely to be fired at you from out of the blue. Random student drop-ins can be prevented, and the easiest way to prevent them is by communicating clearly and unambiguously when you are scheduled to be available. This allows you to be more assertive about carving out the times in your week or term that you have allocated to other things.

Some faculty members say that office hours tie them down and make them feel that they are chained to their desks in the service of their students. But well organized and well publicized office hours don't just make students feel happy and well catered for, they also free you up and help you to manage your time more effectively. It's not for us to say how many hours in the week that you should devote to offering consultation time to your students, but if you are organized and structured, you can find all sorts of ways of ensuring that office hours don't have to be very long to be effective.

You can ask students to drop in in groups, or you can distribute and gather end of lecture questionnaires with questions that prompt students to think about the problems, challenges and issues that they would like to see you about (see sections 1.2, 1.3 and 1.4). By doing this you can pre-empt and shorten the consultation times by being more prepared to help address specific issues identified by specific students.

The office hours rule should be just as clear to students working remotely as they are to their on-campus, full time counterparts. Clarity and consistency with your virtual office hours have just the same effect as those in a conventional university or college environment.

Put the sign on your door, on your website and on your course notes. Publicize your office hours. This gives you permission to locate student consultations into cordoned off parts of your schedule and to carve out protected time for yourself.

3.2 Coaching

> - Coaching focuses on how we challenge, inspire, support, advise and witness students' own development.
> - There are many creative ways in which you can try to build a coaching orientation into your teaching and many ways to prompt a focus on learner performance using simple questions or statements.
> - As you plan or undertake a course or module of teaching, you might consider scheduling some focused coaching or coaching-like sessions into your classroom activity plans.
> - Simple elements of a coaching approach can be integrated into even very large classroom settings.
> - The coaching metaphor is an empowering and motivating one for both teachers and their students.

Students of all ages and backgrounds tend to be guided by a whole range of signals that you send out, not just about your subject but also about various aspects of your orientation and behaviour towards teaching (e.g., Furlong and Maynard 1995). One of the most powerful metaphors for good teaching focuses on the idea of teacher as coach rather than sage (e.g., Adler 1984; Clutterbuck and Megginson 2002). This is an orientation that can help to spread the locus of control for teaching and learner performance more evenly between students and their teachers. If teachers think they have to be the fountains of all knowledge, then the connotations of playing that role creates a sense of dependency between them and their learners (Kolb et al. 2002). If you approach the task of teaching in this way, then you may be tempted always to lead, structure and determine the direction of your students' learning. Alternatively, if you adopt the role of 'coach' then your orientation might be more focused on inviting others to demonstrate their skills allowing you to use your teaching energies to provide supportive inputs in order to help those skills to develop.

The difference is significant and striking. A coaching approach to teaching, wherever this is possible and practical, allows teachers to focus more on the student and their relationship with a topic, which, according to pedagogical wisdom, is a very appropriate place to start (see, for example, Dillon 1988; Bonwell and Eison 1991). Coaching is focused on student performance and competence and it prioritizes interaction with students about their sense of accomplishment. Of course, it is much easier to coach in small group settings than larger ones and so you may be able to practise a coaching approach more successfully in some contexts than others. However, simple techniques can help you to play a coach-like role, even in very large settings. Sometimes it is simply a matter of planning a problem solving task for students to try and then prompting their reflections on the extent to which they believed they were able to solve it. After setting a brief and focused task, you can help students to reflect on their own performance and approaches by using the following kinds of questions:

- How did that go for you?
- Did you find it difficult to . . .?
- Some students automatically try this approach but I suggest that some of you may find X easier to start with . . .

Coaching your students is an engaging and effective alternative to transferring information or to telling them what they should be doing. It involves encouraging students to focus on their own capacities and achievements, being prepared to watch your students carefully and encourage and critique their responses in supportive ways.

3.3 Understanding the benefits of learning communities

- Learning communities are easier to create when you install systems in which students are more likely to interact directly and actively with one another.
- Learning communities make teaching easier and learning more engaged and motivated.
- Good learning communities can help students to learn in first hand ways about the benefits of active citizenship and these principles can reinforce their sense of empowerment and their commitment to communities beyond their classrooms.

We believe that part of anyone's job as a teacher is to introduce people to one another as well as to the topic that they are teaching. Creating a sense of community is not always easy in the sometimes fragmented world of higher and further education (Grant and Knowles 2000), and this may be increasingly the case now that distance learning, part time learning and very large universities and colleges are often the contexts within which education and accreditation takes place. However, anyone who has witnessed the initiation and development of a genuine sense of community within a learning environment, will probably be able to identify some of the important and positive features that this sense of belongingness creates. A community creates unwritten rules that help to guide the activities of its members. And *learning* communities, when healthy and mutually supporting, can create and protect activities that sustain and promote learning.

Effective learning communities bring less able learners on, help learners to communicate actively with one another about their learning tasks and puzzles and sustain dialogue in more general and contextualized ways about issues that are relevant to learning.

Many learners don't necessarily share the values of a learning community, and many feel forced to learn in ways that are isolated and detached from the pleasure of community. We're not suggesting that it is always easy or within your power to transform a fragmented group of individuals into a tight and mutually supporting learning community. However, we do know that there are lots of things you can do to get disparate groups of learners to learn together and to experience the pleasure and effectiveness that their being part of a learning community can bring.

Build your students' sense of collective responsibility. Give them tasks in which they will have to work together in small groups and then collaborate within those small groups with the rest of the class; set up peer partnerships and collectives within the student groups that you teach. Help them to learn about giving and receiving feedback, not just from you but from each other too (see also sections 3.13 and 3.14). Any prompt that encourages and rewards learners for interacting and collaborating more actively with one another in the interests of learning, can contribute to the building of stronger learning communities than might otherwise exist. And if your students feel that they are members of a learning community, your work as a teacher, and theirs as learners, will be supported and enhanced.

Of course, this is also an emphasis that sets the scene for addressing broader aims in educational settings. There is a strong role that educators and teachers can play in helping their societies to foster and to understand such concepts as social cohesion, integration and active citizenship (Jansen et al. 2006). The classroom, real or virtual, may indeed be a good starting point in which to help foster such an understanding among students. To create and encourage participation in learning communities can help students to get used to engaging in negotiating their rights and responsibilities within communities (Sennett 2003), and can provide them with arenas within which to practise some positive principles of citizenship.

3.4 Being honest and humble

- Honest, egalitarian learning environments are healthy places in which to teach and learn.
- Admit when you don't know the answers – your students might be initially surprised, but will respect you and feel more respected.

It's difficult to maintain authority in a classroom, especially when students are bright, demanding, critical and challenging. And yet this is what we want from our students, isn't it? We don't want our students to be docile, passive, disengaged or accepting. Or do we? It has often been said that self-fulfilling prophecies prevail in educational settings. If we expect our students to be docile and unchallenging, then that's what we'll get. If we assume that we know more than anyone else in the class then we may orientate our teaching in a way that encourages or reinforces that assumption. To be humble is part of being a good teacher. Recognizing when we've got it wrong which, let's face it, does happen; remembering that we may not be the cleverest person in the room and making sure that when we see someone cleverer, more informed or more creative than we are, creating room for that voice, are all part of being a good teacher.

Based on evidence, that we have analysed that explores student perceptions of teachers, it seems very unlikely that your students will tend to question your knowledge base (Moore and Kuol 2005). Even in quite critically advanced and challenging learning environments, students seem to accept and assume that their university or college teachers know a great deal about every aspect of every topic that they teach. This assumption can put sometimes intolerable pressure on teachers and also creates an almost definitely unhelpful sense of dependency. It can be very liberating for both you and your students to be completely honest from the very start about your own assessment of your knowledge base. It is both legitimate and refreshing to tell your students that you don't know an awful lot about something. It might feel as if that undermines your credibility, and you might pick and choose exactly how candid you want to be with which student groups, but teachers often report that admissions of knowledge gaps or even weaknesses are good ways of reducing the perceptions of distance between learners and teachers, as well as of making students feel empowered to enquire and discover elements of a topic without feeling that someone else in the room always has a better, more expert, answer.

In the same way, while it may go against the grain, there are really good outcomes to be derived from apologizing when you forget something or admitting when you've done something wrong. At the very worst it will come as a surprise to your students to discover that you can't be expected to be the receptacle of all wisdom and perfection.

3.5 Looking out for learning breakthroughs

- Be on the lookout for your students' 'Aha' moments.
- Help students to see the progress that they have made by keeping records of key learning achievements or encouraging your students to keep their own.

• Be observant about different levels of engagement that students can achieve within your discipline.

One of the great pleasures of teaching comes from witnessing student understanding and achievement. This is particularly satisfying when students have struggled with a difficult skill or problem only to demonstrate, both to you and to themselves, that they have achieved a significant learning breakthrough. This is perhaps the secret delight that teachers derive from the work that they do. Evidence shows that these breakthrough moments are often quite memorable for learners themselves (Armstrong 1998) and often become part of the ways in which particular learning environments and teachers are remembered. Here is how one student recalls their own breakthrough moment in an advanced accounting and finance class:

I really thought that I was stupid – I just couldn't see what everyone else seemed to take for granted. When it finally came to me and I realized that I understood it – well that was huge for me. I realized then that learning happens in fits and starts, it's not even or predictable. Sometimes you're sitting there without a clue, and then unexpectedly, it's clear and you understand.

This is a rich and eloquent statement that reflects many themes in educational, cognitive and learning research. First, the student talks about feeling unable to 'see' something important about what he was learning and, significantly, he attributes that inability to his own stupidity. Indeed other findings have shown that students often use the word stupid or dumb to describe themselves (Seifert 2004), and it seems to be one of those tendencies that creates prohibitive assumptions for them when they are tackling challenging learning activities. He talks about the moment of understanding in a rather passive way ('it finally came to me') but also refers to that moment of understanding as being 'huge'. He recognizes the sometimes stilted pace of learning: that you can make lots of progress in a short time and at other times feel as if your progress is very slow. He talks about breakthroughs in understanding as something unexpected, something that perhaps can't be predicted or scheduled.

All of these insights tell us a lot about the importance of watching out for the 'Aha' moments among your students whenever you can. Even in very big classroom settings, you can look for clues or signals of the times when your students have achieved significant insights. Being on the look out for breakthroughs, pointing out how far students have come by keeping records and demonstrating their progress, can help you not only to spot aspects of their learning and respond to their achievements, but to enhance their knowledge of that progress – to make explicit what they might otherwise not notice about themselves. Insightful teachers don't necessarily have a magic capacity to sense moments of transformation among their students. It's actually a lot simpler than that: teachers who are observant about the signs of cognitive breakthrough will be able to spot basic signals and signs that someone has experienced an important learning moment. And they will be able to respond then in a way that maximizes the benefits and impact of that moment on the learners and on the teaching environment.

3.6 Knowing your students' names

- ·We encourage you to try some techniques that will help you to remember your students' names.
- Calling students by their names can give rise to deeper levels of classroom involvement, provoked by a sense of belonging they might not experience in more anonymous learning contexts.
- Teachers who know and use their students' names tend to open the door to subtly better interactions both within and beyond their lectures and tutorials.

When we discovered that award winning teachers within the University of Limerick were substantially more likely to be nominated by their students simply for knowing the names of everyone in the class, we decided to look into this phenomenon a little more deeply. Clearly, a photographic memory for names, while possibly an impressive party trick, and potentially useful when mingling in social contexts, does not necessarily confer on someone the characteristics of a pedagogical genius. However, given how frequently cited this particular capacity was, and how often it seemed to be directly associated with those teachers that students considered to be outstanding, our investigation sought to find out the reasons for that perception. What we discovered turned out to be quite simple: having someone in a teaching role call you by your name, especially in a large-group formal learning setting, often has a direct effect on a student's sense of belonging and responsiveness. Addressing students by name seems to confer on them a sense of identity and individuality that makes them more likely to respond positively to the material that you are teaching and the context in which you are teaching it.

By knowing your students' names, you simply set the scene for more positive, responsive and appreciative reactions from your students. Of course, as with many teaching orientations, the capacity to remember student names reduces as class size increases (see next section for more about the class size issue), but this doesn't mean that you shouldn't try. Anecdotally, many teachers have shared their strategies for remembering the names of all their students, even in very big student groups. Some ask students to bring a photocopy of their student ID's with them within the first couple of weeks. Others bring a camera, take and print a photo of everyone's face and then ask the class to help them learn everyone's names. Others simply organize legible name badges and ask everyone to keep them visible during the class.

3.7 Treating class size as a political issue

- There is a lot of evidence in education that teacher/student ratios need to be improved.
- Smaller class sizes create better educative environments at all levels and ages, not least in further and higher educational settings.
- Where class sizes are large, work to create opportunities for smaller group interaction.
- Lobby your organization and funders for better student/teacher ratios.

Class size is one of the main moderators of students' perspectives on their learning (e.g., Everston and Randolph 1989). Student/teacher ratio is not just something that affects the quality of student learning – it is also an important political issue. Improvements in this ratio are necessary but not sufficient for improving learning environments.

It's likely that the thorny issue of class size has occurred to you many times as you read the pages of this book, particularly while reflecting on the sections that relate to focusing on students as a key part of any teaching mandate. Indeed, much of the policy and political discourse about higher education globally focuses on how the quality of teaching and learning can be maintained or enhanced in contexts where resources are scarce. The real life teaching and learning settings for most people involve class sizes that are large and diverse, time that is scarce, and pressures that are many.

As we have noted before and as you may have observed in your own settings, students increasingly connect with their education on a part time, distance or modularized basis. The issue of connecting with students and developing meaningful learner relationships remains important, but may for many teachers have become increasingly problematic. People tend to idealize and lament the passing of the continuity, ease and small group settings that tended to characterize traditional university environments (Axtell 2000). And today there are fewer possibilities for small group interactions with our students, mainly because of increasing student numbers in most institutions. Class size *is* an extremely important issue. It will impact on your efforts to teach, even where other emerging resources can be applied to enhancing interaction and communication in larger groups.

It still is the case that students perceptions of satisfying, effective teaching and learning environments are predominantly influenced by class size. Simply put, the smaller the learning group, the easier it seems to be for students to derive benefits from their learning experiences (Angelo and Cross 1993; Race 2001; Moore and Kuol 2005). This observation provides a rationale for doing several things: first, in situations where you do teach to large groups, it is worth planning to organize and structure opportunities within those groups for smaller group interactions. Second, it is worth engaging in collective dialogue about class sizes, and critically challenging the student/teacher ratios within your context with a view to improving them.

Despite the emergence of excellent technological tools that allow us to communicate and teach to large numbers, there still seems to be no substitute for the interested, focused and personal approach that can be achieved when teachers are not overloaded with outlandishly large student numbers. This is a political issue. Lobbying for smaller class sizes has financial and economic implications; is part of the debate about the balance between teaching and research; and is something that requires argument, persuasion and the presentation of convincing evidence about its related benefits and outcomes. If it is an issue that is to receive effective attention, then it needs to be expressed coherently and regularly by teachers and their lobbyists in organized ways. Treat class size as a political as well as a pedagogical issue.

3.8 Helping students with the basic tools of academia

- Students do not arrive at university equipped with knowledge and competence in the tools of academia.
- There may be activities and skills that you take for granted but that your students need explicit instructions and practice in.
- Integrate mini-tutorials to help students to conquer key skills that they will need to perform within your discipline.

Trying to make sense of the 'rules' in college and university is something that students regularly struggle with. You may not deliberately bamboozle or confuse your students, but your increasing familiarity with this academic environment simply allows you to take for granted many of the conventions and expectations that your students are still in the early stages of learning about. A fairly widespread phenomenon in universities has been observed as 'an institutional practice of mystery' (Lillis 2001) in which there are unspoken, unwritten rules that students are expected to absorb easily in the course of their interactions with the institution. But they do not absorb unwritten rules easily, nor are they automatically bestowed with academic competence simply by interacting with and listening to academics in the course of their programmes of study (Lea 2004). Think about the following list, which contains a series of examples of activities within academia:

- plagiarizing
- arguing
- evidencing
- debating
- demonstrating
- writing
- presenting
- referencing
- citing
- quoting
- researching
- reviewing
- searching literature
- experimenting
- testing
- proving
- hypothesizing
- concluding
- summarizing
- analysing
- interpreting.

This is only a sample from what, for you, may be a much longer list of different but connected academic activities in which students are both expected and required to engage. All of the words in the list are likely to be at least somewhat familiar to you. While you may never have been given a precise definition for any of these concepts, surviving in academia for any length of time usually means that you have probably absorbed an implicit understanding of the activities that they involve. Remember that many of your students do not have this implicit knowledge. There are also other more generic and workplace-related skills not on this list that students benefit from developing (see Patterson and Bell 2001). However, we suggest that teachers can improve communication and working assumptions between them and their students by deliberately introducing, defining and explaining these kinds of concepts. For different disciplines, different kinds of activity may be more relevant than others, so it's worth generating your own list from your own teaching and research context. For each activity you identify and prioritize, discuss with students the following:

- How you define the activity – what it means (e.g. plagiarism means writing down words that have been written by someone else and passing them off as your own).
- What the pitfalls and problems associated with that activity might be (e.g. not everyone knows that plagiarism is something to be avoided and that it involves sometimes significant penalties in further and higher educational environments).
- How to orientate yourself towards the activity (or, in the case of plagiarism, to avoid it) – for example, keep records of your sources of information, try to speak and write with your own voice, etc.

Mini-tutorials about key academic skills and conventions are a very useful way in which to punctuate your teaching sessions. There are also many resources and teaching aids that can help you to develop shortcuts and signposts in helping students to build their academic skills set (see, for example, Bean 2001; Moore and Murphy 2005). Also, most academic activities provide strong aids to helping students to develop higher order skills including communicative precision, critical thinking, robust approaches to research and evidence, and a confident capacity to deal with information and ideas. Equipping your students with these academic skills will enhance the currency and impact of your teaching programmes.

3.9 Learning and teaching listening skills

- Focus on listening as well as talking. Allocate time to listening to understand the words spoken by your students rather than always thinking about what to say next.
- Try to make it your priority to understand students' questions, inputs or ideas before either approving or criticizing.
- Take active notes when listening to students, particularly jotting down points of disagreement and agreement when more than one person is talking.
- Ask questions that either (a) help to clarify or explain what others are saying or (b) extend or deepen what others are saying.
- Try not to be too concerned about what you think other people in the group are feeling about the speaker's comments.
- Be aware of each speaker's level of confidence and be ready to support the speaker in articulating their ideas, opinions or knowledge.

(Adapted from Brookfield and Preskill 1999: 96–7)

Good teachers take enormous pride in being able to solve problems, respond to issues, suggest alternatives and guide their students. Many build up an effective repertoire of responses for dealing with student queries, problems, questions and issues. And while that experience and repertoire is useful and efficient, it can sometimes stand in the way of really listening to students, of helping them to articulate what the nature of their concerns or troubles might be. Knee-jerk reactions to student questions are understandable, and where time is scarce, you need to find efficient ways of dealing with student consultations. However, where you don't always have a lot of time, you risk making erroneous assumptions from an initial, stumbling conversation with a student. When you're under pressure yourself, the tendency to direct your students away from you and towards some other organizational support may be strong. And it is easy to redirect learners to a counsellor, student services or some other source of learning support. While rarely driven by malice or ill will, it is still easy to fob students off. And students often say that they feel like they are being a nuisance when approaching their teachers (Patterson 1994). Developing good, deliberate, focused listening skills can help to overcome a misdiagnosis of students' problems, can give rise to students' feeling more understood and cared about. It doesn't necessarily mean that you'll spend centuries in your office having your ear bent by self-indulgent souls who have found an easy target for their extended musings.

Arthur (1996) suggests that in order to learn properly about all aspects of what we do, we need to 'observe, observe, observe: become one with the world'. This may seem like a rather vague instruction, but it has a simple wisdom that can be realized through active listening. Intuition is not something mysterious or superstitious – most of the time it simply means attention to detail. When a student is talking to you, try to sit quietly and be attentive. Listen, and listen well, to everything that they are saying to you. Sometimes students are not aware that they have solutions to their own problems already partly formed within their own minds. If you really listen to them, you can help to show them that their answers often lie inside themselves. Education literally means to lead out. By listening, and by providing a space in which students feel confident and comfortable talking, you can achieve much more in your commitment to teaching than when simply delivering instructions and making students feel like they have to hurry out of your office or your classroom so that you can get on with a long list of much more important things.

Active listening is very difficult (Brookfield and Preskill 1999). It requires energy and a concentrated focus but, paradoxically, it is almost invisible when it is being actively practised. When you are listening you are not saying anything, you are not interrupting, you are not summarizing, paraphrasing or joining in. You are not waiting for everyone else to be quiet so that you can deliver your wisdom. You are not structuring the discussion or defining what is appropriate to talk about or to ask. You are focusing on other people's structures, you are giving people room to articulate both what they understand and what they don't, you are creating a climate in which students are prepared to step forward and actively contribute to the dialogue of learning and insight. Brookfield and Preskill provide guidelines for active listening that you can apply to your own practice, and that you can also use as a guide for coaching your students in developing their own listening skills.

3.10 Understanding learning styles

- Different students learn in different ways, so it is useful to consider varying your own teaching orientation in order to cater for the diversities in learning styles.
- Try to become aware of the different orientations and styles that your students bring to the learning environment, experiment with your own repertoire of teaching and learning activities and prompt them to do the same.

The idea that different students learn in different ways has been central to the development of many strands of educational research in recent decades (see, for example, Kolb 1984; Honey and Mumford 1989; Jensen and DiTiberio 1989; Mumford 1994). And many teachers (even those without any familiarity with learning styles or multiple intelligences theory) find it intuitively appealing to consider that different students learn in different ways. The most popular typology of learning styles comes famously from Kolb (1984), who through his research and analysis has divided learners into four key categories according to the following styles: reflectors, activists, theorists and pragmatists. He suggests that depending on our dominant style, we focus on different aspects of learning, and will thrive in environments in which our styles are both understood and catered for.

Reflectors

Reflectors typically prefer learning situations in which they have the opportunity to think carefully about ideas and concepts in quiet and reflective spaces; to consider a range of possibilities before contributing and acting; and to subject ideas or material to considerable intellectual energy before responding in any overt ways themselves. Reflectors tend to prefer learning situations in which they can write privately about their thoughts on a topic, retreat and reflect on material before being required to respond, and sit quietly with ideas before being asked to solve problems or test their understanding. To cater for reflectors, teachers need to create space and give adequate time to students to think, consider, study, read, explore and analyse.

Theorists

Theorists are learners who are more motivated by exploring how general principles, rules and theories can be derived from specific, concrete experience. Seeing how different aspects of a topic or an issue fit into the whole, attempting to see how parts of a process link together, generating conceptual understanding from concrete experience, deriving key rules from observing dynamics or experiments are all the kinds of activites that theorists tend to value and be good at. Theorists respond in energized ways to the following kinds of questions: what might this mean? What could this demonstrate? What kinds of principles might emerge from this observation? What do all these instances (events/comments/phenomena etc.) have in common and how can these commonalities be linked? Introducing these kinds of questions into learning situations can be very satisfying for theorist type learners.

Pragmatists

Pragmatic learners are those who prioritize what is clearly useful to them. They may be less concerned with theoretical rules or reflective practice, unless there is a pragmatic and immediately useful reason for them. How does this work? Why is this useful? How can I utilize this information/knowledge/idea in ways that will yield interesting or important results for me? Is this likely to come up on the exam? Is this going to provide me with a skill that I can use or that will help me to achieve something important? These are the kinds of questions that can dominate the learning experience of pragmatists. Teachers cater for pragmatic learners when they focus on immediate usability of ideas, the development of usable skills and the demonstration that something is both effective and useful within the learners' context.

Activists

An activist learning style is, unsurprisingly, associated with action. Activist learners prefer to be doing something overt with ideas, concepts, topics and knowledge. Activists are most energized and comfortable when they are talking, making, doing, responding and learning as they go along. Less likely to follow detailed instructions and more likely to try things out, they are happy when they are experimenting with things and feel satisfied if they are getting hands on help when they encounter blocks or barriers that stand in the way of getting things done. They don't mind making mistakes as long as they can be engaged in action, and they need a learning environment that is tolerant and facilitative of the hands on approach to learning new things.

Even if you haven't come across this typology before, you can probably see just from these quick descriptions how responding to the priorities and needs of one type of learner may require a qualitatively different approach from those that might be relevant for others. Kolb and other educational researchers argue that good learning environments recognize the spectrum of learning styles, help learners become versatile in engaging with all four approaches to learning and create opportunities in which action, reflection, theorizing and pragmatism all have an opportunity to manifest themselves in learning processes. Think about how your teaching could cater for these different learning styles or move from one mode of learning to another within the course of a learning session. You can get a good sense of what learning styles and priorities your students have by observing them and listening to the kinds of questions they ask. There are questionnaires that can help to assess student learning styles in a way that might help you to understand the dominant styles and likely priorities of your different student groups (see, for example, Honey and Mumford 1989; Fleming and Mills 1992). Whether you simply decide to use your observational and intuitive skills or whether you decide to adopt a more structured approach to testing your students' learning styles, it is useful to be aware of the general principle that different learners come to learning contexts in different ways, with different concerns and priorities. Responding meaningfully and creatively to these differences is one of the central tasks of an effective teacher in higher educational contexts.

3.11 Understanding multiple intelligences

> - People don't just learn in different ways, they also think differently having different types of intelligence, not all of which are primarily linguistic or numeric.
> - Enhancing learning environments may mean considering a variety of access points to learning, and could involve exploring musical, kinaesthetic, interpersonal and spatial forms of cognitive engagement.
> - Recognizing multiple intelligences can provide another useful framework for catering for diversity among your students.

As well as the idea that there are different learning styles or modes in which people approach their learning tasks, theorists and researchers have also proposed that people bring different types of intellectual competence to bear on their learning (Gardner 1998; Barrington 2004). Multiple intelligence theory, while controversial in some educational circles (e.g., Klein 1998) suggests that rather than there being one type of intelligence (i.e., that associated with the concept traditionally known as IQ or intelligence quotient) people can be intelligent in different ways. Gardner and colleagues at Harvard University, through their research, have challenged the persistent idea that there is one kind of intelligence and that the extent to which we possess this defines our ability to learn. He argues that most people possess a spectrum of different kinds of intelligence but that within that spectrum, we each have our own distinctive cognitive and learning preferences. Furthermore, he argues that many academic and educative settings focus on a limited range of intelligence and cognitive preferences, thereby implicitly discriminating against people who have approaches that lie predominantly beyond or outside the ways in which people traditionally teach. Perhaps, as Gardner has argued, it is time for teachers to reconsider, experiment with and redefine our assumptions of intelligence. For Gardner, intelligence can be defined in the following ways:

- The ability to solve everyday problems that are relevant to our lives.
- The capacity to come up with new problems and questions.
- The ability to make something or offer a service that is seen as important within the cultures and societies in which we live.

Given that educational environments are becoming more multicultural and more diverse, it is useful to start thinking in more inclusive and culturally relevant ways about what constitutes performance and effectiveness in learning or, more crucially, what the signals about effective learning might be. The seven kinds of intelligence that Gardner has identified are:

1 *Linguistic intelligence.* The capacity to articulate ideas through language and to express complex meaning using words and sentences.
2 *Logical–mathematical intelligence.* The ability to calculate, quantify, reason using hypotheses and propositions, to come to logical conclusions based on a rational review of evidence and information.
3 *Spatial intelligence.* The ability to visualize and think in three dimensional ways. The ability to navigate, design and to code and decode visual depictions, maps, plans of physical space in accurate ways.
4 *Bodily-kinaesthetic intelligence.* The ability to work with body and hands with precision and detail. The ability to manipulate objects, tools and artefacts in artful ways.
5 *Musical intelligence.* Sensitivity to, appreciation of and ability to create melody, music, rhythm, pace and cadence through the manipulation of sound, voice and instrument.
6 *Interpersonal intelligence.* Empathy, understanding and ability to respond appropriately and positively to other people. The ability to create positive interpersonal environments.
7 *Intrapersonal intelligence.* Self-awareness and the ability to use that awareness for self-development, skills building and life choices.

Even if you have never seen this list before, it is probably easy for you to see that academic environments tend to favour and facilitate the first two types of intelligence (linguistic and logical–mathematical) more strongly than any of the others. And yet many of the most compelling (and, we think, interesting) ideas about innovation in teaching and education strongly encourage teachers to recognize and to find avenues for developing the other forms of intelligence outlined in the list above. There are now tested innovations that have been shown to generate energized and positive learning outcomes by tapping into different kinds of intelligence (see, for example, Marcic 1989; Campbell et al. 1996; Moore and Ryan 2006).

Of course, you need to guard against the temptation to turn your teaching into a hyperstimulated, fragmented, incoherent set of experiences that confuse and bombard your students without necessarily covering the required curriculum, while also remembering that real learning can be unstructured and chaotic (Larsen 2004). Well designed teaching interventions that recognize the different kinds of competencies that different learners bring with them can transform and refresh your approach, particularly if your teaching feels stale or in need of a more active, dynamic, diverse set of orientations. Simple ways of integrating such approaches to learning orientations and capacities might include the following:

- Having a class debate or carrying out role play and negotiation in groups (e.g., Race 2001). This can enhance and facilitate both linguistic and interpersonal competence.
- Audio and or videotaping individual performances and presentations (e.g., Angelo and Cross 1993). When accompanied by sensitive and accurate coaching, this can enhance intrapersonal competence.
- Introducing music into the classroom, either as part of the backdrop of a learning environment (to enhance reflection and change the class climate or group dynamics) or by having an active experience involving the making of music (to generate connections and collaboration between people). See for example, Moore and Ryan (2006).
- Visualization and sketching exercises to help learners to apply spatial, conceptual or mapping skills to ideas and concepts that you are teaching (e.g., Scribner and Anderson 2005).
- Activities that involve building, modelling, making, fixing or crafting where students are required to engage their bodies and hands as well as their brains in classroom tasks (e.g., Kezar 2004) – in order to facilitate bodily-kinaesthetic competencies.

You might already have an idea about what might be most appropriate or useful for the subjects and themes that you teach. You may decide to try a couple of new ways of creating access points to learning that material. Even if you don't, it's useful to be aware that students don't think or learn in identical ways and that diversity is a given, even if it's not immediately obvious. This recognition might have subtle and positive effects on the ways in which you orientate yourself towards your work as a teacher.

3.12 Helping students to cope with stress and pressure

> - It's not your role to eliminate stress for your students, but you can help them to cope more effectively with it.
> - Don't be too surprised at emotional reactions from your students, particularly close to exams or key assignments – be prepared.
> - Help students to put stressful situations in perspective, but also don't trivialize or dismiss their concerns.
> - Be vigilant for more serious signs of anxiety and in those situations be prepared to call for professional help.

When students cross the threshold of any university in the world for the first time, they enter an unfamiliar domain, a domain that will make demands on them that they have not experienced before

(Ridley 2004: 91)

Evidence from all over the world suggests that student stress is a global phenomenon. Students often report feelings of being overwhelmed, unsupported and misunderstood, and that these kinds of experiences create stress and anxiety often at the times in their student lives when they need to be coping at their best (Knox 2005). In addition to this, teachers don't always feel responsible for student stress, nor do they feel they can necessarily do anything about it. And yet, when students report to us (and to others) who their best teachers were, they often talk about the role that great teachers played, not in eliminating stress from their lives but rather in helping them to manage it successfully. It is not your job to shield students from difficulty or challenge. They will encounter frustration and confusion. They will suffer from setbacks and unexpected crises. This is simply the stuff of life and students need to encounter this just as much as all of us do. But it is possible for you to play a key and potentially transformative role in your students' lives by recognizing when stress levels are reaching a dangerous level and by providing students with simple tools for managing their stress with positive effect. Here are some guidelines that might help you to consider how best you can do this:

1 Don't trivialize. The things that cause significant stress to students may mystify or bemuse you. Dynamics that you are very accustomed to are potentially very problematic for them. Don't respond to their concerns by telling them not to worry or that everything is going to be fine. Give them strategies to respond effectively to what is worrying them.
2 From time to time, emotional interchanges are to be expected. Don't panic.

One tearful interchange with a student should not necessarily lead you to call in the expert counsellors. When students talk to you about difficult issues, they may cry or show other signs of distress and upset. On a practical level, it's useful to have a box of tissues in your office so that you can provide recognition and assistance for their distress. Don't be afraid of their tears – it's often a sign that they see you as providing a safe place within which to vent their feelings. Recognizing their distress and helping them to articulate it can often be just what a student needs to explore and gain control over what's distressing them.

3 Know the signs for referral to expert counsellors. If you notice that a student seems regularly tearful, withdrawn, upset or angry, it may be a sign that there are protracted issues that might need more expert emotional support and assistance. It's not always easy to make the call, but being aware of students and their issues can help you to respond appropriately to the difficulties that they face.

3.13 Giving positive feedback

- Students tend to thrive on positive information about their performance. The more detailed and specific this feedback is, the more likely they will be able to use that feedback to continue to perform and to enhance their performance in the future.
- Be vigilant about opportunities to observe and reinforce excellent performance among your students.

It is satisfying to come across student work that is excellent or exemplary. When you've given instructions that students follow carefully – when you've encouraged creative thinking and when that's exactly what your students engage in – when you see a well formed, considered and beautifully argued piece of written work, or massive improvements in a student's capacity to comprehend and articulate something challenging or difficult – these are key learning moments that we should not let pass without some firm endorsement to signal to those students that they have achieved something important and have earned your positive response as a result. The kinds of responses to good student performance or accurate responses to difficult questions might include the following kinds of verbal endorsements: 'Well done!' 'Exactly right'. If students provide answers or responses that are not completely accurate, but demonstrate that they are moving towards understanding and articulating something clearly, it's still good to encourage them by adopting a positive orientation. In those situations you might try the following: 'Almost right,' 'I think you're getting there,' 'Not quite it, but I think I know where you're coming from'.

Remember that it's just as unhelpful for students not to know that they've done well as it is not to know that they've done badly. In addition the reasons for their performance need to be clearly explicated and communicated. Generally, the more warmly and personally you can send this message, the more of an impact it will have on your learners. 'Well done,' might sound condescending and patronizing, but evidence suggests that this is unlikely to be the way that it is received. Rather a response like that encourages, bestows confidence and makes it more likely that that student will hazard another answer, will stay switched on and will be motivated to seek out further positive feedback – and they will do this by working hard within the learning environment that you are helping to create.

But be cautious about feedback that is too positive or, at times, inappropriately so. Although positive feedback as a rule is both more satisfying and more motivating, when inappropriately delivered it can lead to a false sense of security that is not in your students' best interests if they are underperforming in certain ways. Don't rush to agree with your students or to endorse what they have said/written/performed. Where they have missed some essential elements, where they have answered a question only partially, omitted important aspects of a particular issue or missed a learning target completely, you need to tell them clearly and honestly the ways in which they could have performed more effectively. You may be focusing on certain indicators of performance that might include the need for more clarity, precision, critical insight, accuracy, informed basis or evidence. Being able to identify the strengths of your students' learning is professionally very satisfying. However, being overeager to congratulate and agree, even if they have missed something, can give rise to a poor understanding on their part about important gaps that they may need to address.

3.14 Giving negative feedback

- Tell your students about their strengths as well as weaknesses. Go into as much detail about the strengths of their work as you can.
- Only then, move on to showing them how they could do better.
- Project a belief in your students. Try assuming that they have already worked hard (even if you suspect they haven't) to produce their work. Be a champion of their work.
- Don't condescend to students. Be honest with them while always acknowledging your subjectivity. Develop a good enough rapport with them so that

you can say straight and tough things like: 'I think this could have been much better,' without them feeling this is the end of the world.

- Encourage your students to listen but also to retain control. If students are panicking or arguing, they are often blocking good feedback that could help them to be better at what they are trying to learn. See Elbow and Belenoff (2000) for a more detailed discussion of the importance of understanding the impact of feedback on learners.
- Try not to stand on a pedestal. There's probably already enough of a power distance between you and your students without reinforcing it during times when you're giving them feedback that might be difficult for them to absorb and accept. Teachers who recall their own struggles and failures often reassure students and build their confidence in important ways.

It is a psychological fact that people don't like to get negative feedback. Positive feedback is easier to deliver and it's comfortable, enjoyable and socially endorsing to see it have such pleasant effects on students. However, you do no service to students by giving false positive feedback, a temptation that looms especially when you are tired or frazzled and don't want to engage in the more difficult encounter that involves telling a student that their performance is somehow under par. This short section will outline some of the common responses to negative feedback that your students may display and it will provide you with some useful pointers about how you can craft negative feedback in ways that are more likely to yield positive responses from your students.

Students can find even the slightest indication of failure or mistake stressful and worrying (e.g., Honkimaki et al. 2004). Negative feedback can hurt them and make them feel incompetent and sometimes hopeless (see, for example, Spandel and Stiggins 1990). And in turn, this experience can cause them to respond to negative feedback in a range of unhelpful ways. It's worthwhile being aware of their natural responses to negative feedback so that in your own teaching you can temper and pre-empt the normal but less helpful reactions to critical feedback that you might provide them with about their work.

Denial

Students can refuse to accept that your feedback is valid. They can argue with you about your interpretations of what they have done. They can presume that you haven't understood their perspective or approach and they can refuse then to respond to aspects of what you are saying that could help them to improve their performance. The best way to pre-empt a response of denial from your students is, as far as possible, to try to create a safe, undefensive learning environment. This usually means being prepared to be a coach (see section 3.2) before acting as a judge.

Fixation

Unless you differentiate between important and less important aspects of student performance, they can become fixated about aspects of their learning that may not be as important as they think. Bean (2001) recommends differentiating between higher order and lower order concerns among learners and communicating the difference clearly and carefully. Basic rules of writing include bibliographic conventions, issues of grammar and spelling, etc. But if ideas and structures are not sound, conforming to these lower order concerns may not make much difference in the context of student performance. To help students avoid becoming fixated on small issues, communicate your learning priorities clearly and unambiguously to them. See also more about this issue in sections 6.2, 6.3 and 6.4.

Withdrawal

If students find negative feedback intolerably stressful, they may engage in behaviour that is even more extreme than denial and fixation. Even the most normal and well adjusted students have found ways of withdrawing from their studies, either psychologically or physically. This often happens in response to an experience that has made them feel somehow deeply incompetent or unable to engage with the rigours of their course of study. Psychological withdrawal represents a shutting down of engagement, motivation or energy and can mean that students will significantly underutilize their skills, only doing what is needed to achieve a bare pass, or allowing themselves to slip so far behind the course requirements that they end up failing. If students feel that they are not capable of understanding or overcoming blocks to their learning, these are the kinds of responses that they risk reacting with. The extreme version of withdrawal involves dropping out completely (Tinto 1993). To help students avoid these types of responses, teachers need to focus on providing them with positive strategies along with a belief in their students' abilities to activate those strategies. This is the difference between saying: 'You've got that wrong,' and 'You've got this wrong, but here are the interesting and actionable ways in which you can get it right'. Always be prepared to deliver the second part of the pedagogical message in the face of student failure. No matter how many times you give this advice, remember that the student you are looking at at any given point may be receiving this message for the first time. They need to hear it loud and clear: they need to know how and why they have failed (on, say, an assignment/essay/problem) but crucially, they need to know the steps they can take to succeed in future (Zinsser 1988). Unless they clearly hear that part of the message, they are at risk of giving up.

Recognition

The best response that students can give to underperformance is a recognition that there were gaps in their understanding or performance, and a resolution to do something active and positive about those gaps. To learn an undefensive, performance orientated response to criticism is something that will support their professional development not just in the short term but right through their lives. Developing a positive repertoire of responses to critical comments is a skill that students really benefit from. Teachers can help them to do this simply by providing safe spaces in which to consider their performance, by providing signposts to enhancing aspects of their performance, by projecting a positive belief in students' capacity to respond positively, and by endorsing and encouraging those responses once they emerge (see also section 6.3).

Good teachers are aware of the possible impact that feedback has on their students. When you consider the effect that feedback has on you (from student surveys, peer observation reports, journal reviewers, friends and foes) you can probably identify with the fact that certain levels of discomfort are associated with receiving information about your performance. Indeed, while the stakes can feel high for teachers when they are grappling with performance feedback of any kind, it is entirely possible that they feel even higher for students doing the same thing. Students tell us in particular that written feedback can feel much more hard hitting than that delivered in a conversation (e.g., Bean 2001) and, generally, the higher the stakes (e.g. the closer a student is to a key deadline or the extent to which a piece of work affects their overall grade or grades), the more difficult it will be for them to respond rationally to feedback, particularly if it is negative. To control the kinds of panic responses that students display (e.g. ignoring feedback, denying feedback, distorting feedback or overreacting to feedback), it pays to get into the habit of delivering negative feedback carefully and sensitively.

3.15 Dealing with indiscipline and lack of interest

- Knee-jerk blaming of students for poor classroom climates can add to your frustration. Talk to them after class, discuss their experiences and see if there is some way you can work together to create more positive classroom climates.
- There are times in which your students will probably have to listen quietly to you as you speak – remember they can sometimes find this difficult, disengaging and passive so try to balance didactic sessions with more active modes of learning.
- Very difficult or aggressive behaviour is not sustainable either within the classroom or outside it. If you feel threatened or harassed, you need to respond with the processes and protections of your institution.

Even the most committed teacher's enthusiasm can be tested by some of the realities of teaching. Classroom indiscipline and student lack of interest can be particularly soul destroying. Effective education demands a partnership between the teacher and student, with both needing to demonstrate dedication and commitment. As the lecturer, you are responsible for taking the lead in creating a climate maximally conducive to learning. Most students will respond positively to this but it is probably inevitable at times that some will lack interest and commitment. If discipline problems in the classroom do occur, it will almost definitely have a negative influence on your teaching as well as on the learning environment of the other students. Difficulties with student behaviour in class need to be swiftly and firmly addressed.

In an idealized setting indiscipline can be most comprehensively addressed by, first, determining its root cause. For example, extreme student dissatisfaction/frustration at a course/course element may manifest itself through mild indiscipline (Rutherford 1991). Therefore, should you feel it appropriate, when talking to the disruptive individual(s), enquire if the root cause of the difficulty is related to a professional educational matter over which you have influence.

Your reaction to such occurrences should be professional and proportionate. Most instances of indiscipline are likely to be relatively minor. Examples of behaviour that you might find difficult or challenging to deal with include the following: lateness, interrupting or active inattention and hostility (see Appleby 1990). Sorcinelli (1990) suggests several practical ways of responding to these kinds of behaviours. They include (a) making direct eye contact with the disruptive students and pausing the class – this can sometimes be enough to get the students to focus their attention again; (b) asking a question of someone sitting directly beside the disruptive student – this can create a proximal focus that might serve to re-engage him/her; (c) simply asking the interrupters to stop; (d) talking to the student after class and positively restating the ground rules of class behaviour.

On occasion, however, difficult behaviour can be more severe and persistent. In such instances more decisive action is likely to be warranted, such as the immediate issue of a verbal or written warning, or the initiation of some sort of disciplinary action. In this context it is important for you to be familiar with university policy/procedures with regard to such issues. Such policies and procedures are usually included in a handbook of academic administration. It is also good practice to remind the students of their obligation to behave in a professional manner in accordance with the appropriate university 'code of behaviour'. This can, for example, be incorporated into each course/module information pack provided to students at the beginning of each course.

Another negative classroom norm occasionally characteristic of some students is that of disengagement. This is usually easy to spot, being betrayed by student facial expressions, body language or an obvious lack of engagement with the subject matter. Again lack of interest can be triggered by many factors, many of which you can do something about. Measures considered to counteract disinterest can include:

- Encouraging/promoting greater class participation during the module by increased interaction with the students (e.g. asking questions or setting up student 'buzz groups' in which students are clustered into smaller groups of three or four to focus on a particular issue and then report back to the larger group through a spokesperson from the group). See also section 2.6.
- Backing up more abstract concepts presented with practical illustrative examples.
- Fine-tuning the course content to ensure its relevance is immediately obvious to each student cohort present. Many subjects/courses are taken by multi-cohorts of students. Those cohorts undertaking degree programmes closely aligned to your specific subject often display greater interest/commitment than those undertaking degree programmes in which your subject is more peripheral.

On the rare occasion that a students' behaviour feels overtly hostile or threatening, it is important that you minimize the impact of this on you and on other students and get assistance from heads of departments, human resources or student services.

3.16 Helping students to deal with poor performance

- Instil in your relationship with the students the promise that you will provide supportive feedback and analysis of their work. This will encourage students to engage with you.
- Help underperforming students to reflect upon the root cause of their poor performance and how they might take their own steps to address it.
- Try to allocate particular time slots to students who have failed or underperformed on your assignments/projects/exams. Going through the student's work with them and explaining clearly the main reasons why they have underperformed can be a very simple way of transforming student approaches to the challenges you set for them.

Correcting exams or student coursework can be a sobering experience, particularly if students underperform in ways that you did not predict or expect. As disappointing as this is for you, it can be doubly so for the students concerned. Poor performance will not only affect their immediate overall academic standing but can trigger self-doubt and a lack of confidence in their own ability. This, in turn, can increase the chances of future poor performance.

Poor performance can be caused by a number of factors, including:

- Lack of student commitment or interest.
- Lack of student academic ability.
- Some negative occurrence in the student's life (e.g. family bereavement).
- Poor exam assessment technique.
- Poor course delivery on your part.
- Poor exam/assessment design, for example where an exam or assessment does not reflect the emphasis and content of the course covered.
- Lack of student understanding of your expectations as examiner/assessor.

Reflective practice, including student feedback, will be important in analysing if your teaching contributed to poor performance and, more importantly, how to minimize this in the future. Lack of student understanding of your expectations as an examiner is a point worth considering a little further, as it is less obvious than most of the other potential causes, and yet can be a real issue. Most students will be taught several courses by several different lecturers at any one time. Each lecturer may have their own educational philosophy which will impinge not only upon course delivery but also upon examination and marking. Examination ethos and expectations may – and most probably will – differ significantly from lecturer to lecturer. For example, some examiners prefer short, very focused answers, while others prefer broader answers; some place greater emphasis upon the provision of evidence of significant background reading than others; etc. Therefore it is important for you to make as clear to the students as possible your attitude/expectations in terms of coursework/exam requirements (see also Chapter 6). Often such issues can most conveniently be included as part of an initial course information pack. Also worthy of inclusion in such information packs is a list/description of 'Common reasons as to why students can perform poorly in my exams,' or 'Points to remember when completing coursework/an exam'. With experience you will find that each year a proportion of students fare less well than they could have because, for example, their answer wandered off the point, they didn't apportion appropriate time to each question, they failed to provide specific examples illustrating a general principle, etc. In our experience many students also find it particularly helpful if a sample question and associated answer template or sample answer is provided, to help them to interpret your expectations.

By adopting a broadly supportive and proactive role you will not only help the student come to terms with their poor performance but, more importantly, increase the likelihood of improvement and confidence in the future.

3.17 Being emotionally aware

- Effective learning requires emotional as well as intellectual engagement.
- Be prepared to encounter emotional responses from your students, particularly at certain times of the semester, and consider the ways in which you might respond sensitively and constructively to their emotional states.
- Reflect on your own emotions and how they might affect your approaches to teaching.

Learning and teaching are matters of the heart as well as the head. This is sometimes difficult for teachers to recognize and respond to. How teachers and students feel has an impact on how they teach and how they learn. Ignoring the emotional dimensions of learning not only cuts us off from very important pieces of pegagogical information, but also it bypasses some of the most powerful ways in which learning can be accessed and experienced by students and their teachers. Being emotionally aware doesn't imply that you need to be particularly emotionally expressive. It means simply that you commit to being sensitive to the kinds of emotions that are influencing your behaviours and the kinds of emotional impact your teaching activities and interactions might have on your students. Similarly, an emotionally aware teacher does not demand that students express or display their emotional states. They don't foster environments in which emotional outbursts or strongly emotion-laden responses are the norm. Indeed, such an environment would probably not be a good climate in which to learn. It is important that teaching environments are characterized by strong boundaries between private and public experiences and that norms keep people safe and protected – not exposed. However, when you are working with learners, you need occasionally to be prepared to be able to cope with moments during which emotional responses bubble to the surface. It is important that you feel equipped to deal responsively and appropriately with such an experience in a way that respects both you and your students.

Goleman (2000), Moore and Murphy (2005) and Moore and Kuol (2007) have been among many writers in education who recognize and endorse the importance of the concept of emotional intelligence in learning environments. The characteristics of emotional intelligence are simple: they include emotional self-awareness (understanding how you are feeling and how that may affect what you think and how you behave); emotional control (being able to contain and control emotions in a way that gives rise to positive outcomes); social skills (understanding the impact of your behaviour on other people's emotional states); and empathy (being able quickly to guage, appreciate and respond appropriately to how other people are feeling).

It is often very difficult for teachers to pick up the emotional pulse of a class, or to explain the reasons for certain classroom dynamics. Students at different times of their learning journeys will experience sometimes very intense and extreme emotions. Just like all of us, they are subject to the human experiences of fear, guilt, anxiety, anger, joy, happiness, relief and many other emotions besides. We think it is important to accept this and to be prepared for these feelings to manifest themselves in some way in our learning settings. As Goleman (2000) asserts, once you can name and respond to emotionally difficult or intense feelings, even if you're teaching what you consider to be a very cognitive subject, then you will be more likely to adopt a more holistic, effective and responsive orientation towards your students.

3.18 Involving students in the teaching of their classes

- Getting students to collaborate in the teaching of their own class heightens their sense of status and involvement and is likely to give rise to active, engaged responses from learners.
- Having students engage in the research necessary to teach well can provide you with new ideas, directions and avenues to enhance your own teaching.
- You don't always have to be the source of knowledge and wisdom – handing some of that responsibility over to your students, even for small portions of teaching, is good for both teachers and learners.

There is a lament often heard among teachers in further and higher education. It relates to the perception by teachers that students are too passive (Jackson and Prosser 1989), that they do not take enough ownership of their learning, that they are not nearly as autonomous or self-directed as we would like them to be. An assumption of dependency exists between teachers and their students, with the former calling the shots, directing the action and determining the features and dynamics of learning, while the latter sit back and wait for their brains to be filled with information rather like buckets are filled with water. W.B Yeats said that education is not the filling of a bucket, it is the lighting of a fire. In many teaching contexts teachers are often reluctant to step back and provide students with the room they sometimes need to operate in self-directed and active ways (see McBrien 2006). Many teachers were taught by people who delivered lectures/classes in very conventional and didactic ways, and where this is the case the likelihood that they will replicate this style is high. However, if you feel that your students could be more active and more engaged in the learning of the subjects that you are teaching, then there are quite simple ways in which you can involve and consult with them about the teaching of your class. Consider experimenting with the following:

1 Have your students research an area of the course that you feel you know least about. Explain the nature of your own struggles and see if students can respond actively to the questions or concerns that you pose.
2 In smaller groups, with the support of structured guidelines, invite students to prepare a learning session on a particular topic. Give them a shorter time frame within the context of a longer teaching slot, and then use the learning session that they have led to guide the discussion for the remainder of the class.
3 Coach students about the principles of effective information gathering and literature searches. Help them to become familiar with the layout of the library and where they can find key sources of information. And provide coaching about the best ways in which they can search the internet for sound, evidence-based sources of information and guidance (see also section 3.2).

By setting these kinds of tasks for your students you create a much stronger chance that they will engage actively and autonomously with your course, that they will get to know each other by working together and that they will have memorable and positive learning experiences.

3.19 Helping your students develop sound goals

- The emotional impact of 'good goals' creates optimism, the mobilization of energy and the focus that it takes to undertake a challenging programme of study.
- Even a small amount of coaching in goal setting tends to make students more likely to decide and know exactly what they want to learn during each study session; to test the achievement of their defined tasks; to select tasks that are neither easy nor impossible; and to achieve their defined tasks within the time frame that they have allocated to it.

It's worth helping students to think about and generate goals for themselves – exploring issues associated with time and tasks and helping them to scope out realistic learning plans. More generally, adopting a goal orientated approach to teaching can provide focus, concentration and motivation among your student groups. The SMART framework (see, for example, Moore and Murphy 2005) is a useful tool that can help you to create appropriate goals for your students and ultimately help them to generate their own learning and work goals. SMART stands for: Specific (learning or study goals should be specific and detailed so that students can apply their energies and attention in focused ways to particular ideas, concepts or activities); Measurable (students can benefit from designing their learning session in ways that allow them to test themselves at the end of a task to see if they have achieved what they planned); Ambitious (goals should be brave enough to stretch students capacities a little); Realistic (tasks that students set for themselves should reflect realistic and achievable goals, and they should be encouraged to understand the 'size' of different parts of their course so that they can apportion time and energies appropriately); and Time-bound (students should be encouraged to specify and become familiar with the different time slots available to them and to create their own deadlines within which various planned goals will be achieved).

3.20 Making learning more fun

- There are many different options available to you for teaching. Introducing an element of surprise enhances overall levels of attention and engagement among your students.
- Don't introduce gimmicks or tricks for their own sake, but be prepared to think creatively about different techniques and activities that might activate your students.
- Students learn through play, positive competition, idea exchange and action. Consider introducing these elements into your own teaching strategies.

Many teachers report that they didn't have the greatest role models when they were students themselves. Too often they experienced dry, monotone, purely didactic and often uninspiring learning contexts. If this has been your experience as a learner, it's sometimes difficult to know where to start to make learning fun for your own students. But once you start trying to inject fun into your teaching, you'll find that one interesting or engaging idea gives rise to another, and soon you will have built up a repertoire of interactions, techniques, tricks and interventions that can help students really participate with motivation and excitement in your classes, lectures, tutorials or seminars.

Making learning fun creates a love of your subject among your students that may otherwise be very difficult to achieve. Some ideas for making learning fun include the following (but remember, once you've tried a few of these ideas, you'll undoubtedly start to think of many more techniques for yourself that suit your own subject and that are ideal for your learning environments):

- Use *icebreakers* so that students can get to know each other, become used to interacting and be more likely to interact with each other about your subject outside of formal class time. This is particularly important in the early weeks of your time together or if you're doing once-off teaching with groups normally taught by others. Simple icebreakers involve five minute discussion sessions, in smaller groups or pairs at the beginning of a teaching session, in which students can be instructed fo find out more about each other, answer key questions, write about a topic or solve a puzzle.
- Introduce *a physical activity*. This is anything that involves students getting up from their seats and doing something physically active. Pin signs or pictures up on a wall and have your students move closer to them to examine, analyse or discuss them, get students to move around briefly if their attention seems to be flagging or they look tired and listless, design a treasure hunt and have students find objects you have hidden that are linked to the topic of the day.
- Make ideas, concepts or course content *three dimensional*. Unless they work in labs or out on fieldwork, students from all backgrounds and subjects often see things only in two dimensions when they're learning – even if visual illustrations are good replicas, they're often not in 3D. Helping students to understand something may involve bringing a real object into the classroom or encouraging them to make objects that reflect or symbolize something that they are learning about. It might take a little more planning and preparation on your part, but a third dimension can really help to bring something alive.
- *Play*. If you observe people when they're playing, you'll probably notice that levels of focus and concentration are high, people are engaged in the moment, interested in performing well, but generally unselfconscious and absorbed. These are ideal conditions for learning (see Mitchell 1998). Play is one of the ways in which students' own intrinsic, natural propensity for learning can manifest itself (Piaget 1951). Teachers who really want their students to learn and are encountering difficulties in motivating them can benefit from introducing games into the classroom. Games must be designed carefully to ensure that they relate to the learning objectives associated with what you are teaching, but again some thought and planning can create an interactive, visual, collaborative and engaged atmosphere that gets students thinking, solving problems and working hard.
- *Introduce unexpected or surprising elements into your teaching.* Without overwhelming or confusing your students, it is possible to keep them engaged by doing unexpected things regularly. Howard Gardner has reminded us for many years that different students have different access points to learning (see also section 3.11). Some prefer to learn visually, others kinaesthetically, others numerically, others linguistically. Gardner encourages teachers to

remember that not every student learns in the same way and has recommended that teaching should accommodate different types of learning within the same classroom setting. Consider the ways in which you can create diverse methodologies in your classroom. If you cater only for one kind of learning orientation, then the experience can become mundane and bland for everyone. But if there is an air of unpredictability about what you do – if your students are never quite sure what kind of experience they are going to have, or what kinds of props you are going to use in your efforts to teach them, their overall experience is likely to be more interesting, more curiosity-inducing and more fun. Don't be reluctant to use pictures, stories, models, puzzles, colours, music, role plays or even drama in your classrooms. This is just as relevant for advanced learners in universities as it is for very young children. Learners start to own their learning more actively and more proudly if they are having fun while you're teaching them. They may have to plough through difficult or tedious parts of your course, but if the promise of an interesting or novel experience lurks in the air ready to pounce at any moment, even the tedious parts of the course can become more bearable and memorable.

3.21 Helping students to rise to challenges and rewarding risk-taking

> - There are times when students will look for assistance and support when it may be more important for them to go it alone, or proceed at least without expert help.
> - Sometimes very helpful and obliging teachers can make the mistake of bending over backwards for students who perhaps need a bit of a push to generate their own outlines, to search for their own literature, to come to their own conclusions and to take their own risks.

It's not always your job to make life easy for your students. As we've noted, you can't prevent them from feeling stressed at least occasionally and you can't shield them from the challenges of academic life. They are on their own quest to survive and to thrive in what is necessarily a challenging and sometimes problematic environment. However, it is important to take responsibility for not making their lives impossible, their studies unsustainable or their experience impoverished in some fundamental ways. It is useful to see college and university as safe places in which students can gain understanding, test and develop their skills, and learn to rise to challenges in a protected and supported environment. It is hard to provide this type of environment, particularly when your own time has to be carefully managed, and the pressures of your career development may make you feel that you need to restrict the amount of time you devote to helping students, certainly outside the formal classroom situation, if not within it. However, there are practical ways in which you can help students to rise to the challenges of their academic environment in general, and of the tasks, assignments and questions that you set them.

Part of your students' learning journey at university involves them becoming self-directed and autonomous within their field of study. Whether you are teaching young school leavers or mature students, or most probably a mix of both, the importance of autonomous learning should be something that you emphasize, and its existence should be something that you encourage. Too much instruction or direction can undermine the goal of independence and self direction. You need to be able to work out when to tell students that certain decisions are up to them.

Students who do things differently, who hazard an answer to a difficult question, or who otherwise step outside the boundaries of what you expect or require in the interests of learning need to be rewarded and endorsed. Setting a norm within your classrooms and teaching spaces that allows students to take risks, even when those risks lead to failure and identifies what was brave or commendable about that risk, is a way of helping to create a culture in which students will feel comfortable with 'stepping forward' in order to learn, to develop, to contribute, to participate and to grow.

3.22 Generating enthusiasm and nourishing curiosity

- Nourishing curiosity among students is something that is not necessarily the preserve of naturally gifted orators.
- There are simple tricks you can use to keep them paying attention to your line of argument, explanations or expositions.
- Using phrases to say that you're going to reveal gradually the elements of a problem or an issue can maintain the attention and curiosity of students in very simple ways.

It is arguable whether enthusiasm is a quality that feeds good teaching. You can be an enthusiastic teacher without being particularly effective. And you can be a very effective teacher without being particularly enthusiastic. However, there is enough evidence in the literature on teaching to argue that enthusiasm does have a role to play in engaging students and in developing among them a positive orientation towards the learning of the subjects that you teach (Axtell 2000).

There are easy, small and actionable techniques you can use to turn a rather dull, didactic delivery of material into an engaged, curious and stimulating one. Here are some strategies that you could inject into the pacing and language of your lectures that serve to do this:

- Signalling importance: 'As you'll see in a few minutes, this element of the equation is vital' (maths).
- Indicating 'big/dramatic' events: 'As it turns out, the way in which the whole thing ended was much more disastrous than anyone had predicted, but before I tell you about that, here are a few useful facts' (history).
- Encouraging engagement: 'In some ways, you'll realize at the end of this that this particular question leads us to a number of possible answers for you to judge the merits and demerits of for yourselves' (philosophy).
- Indicating controversy: 'I'm going to tell you about a couple of very controversial experiments that could not be replicated today but which tell us a lot about some of the fundamental aspects of human behaviour' (psychology).
- Focusing on student action: 'When you do this experiment in the second half of this class, all of these characteristics will need to be attended to' (science).

3.23 Being creative

- Helping students to speak with their own voices, to start with their own understanding and perspective on issues that you are teaching, to express themselves without fear of censure or inappropriateness, may be a good starting point to facilitate their creative engagement with topics, material, ideas, problems and knowledge in your subject areas.
- Being a creative teacher sometimes requires being prepared to live within the sometimes extreme paradoxes of creative action, in order to bring learning environments alive both for ourselves and for our students.

If I had to express in one word what makes [creative people] different from others, it's complexity. They show tendencies of thought and action that in most people are segregated. They contain contradictory extremes.

(Cziksentmihalyi 1996)

Creative people while often extremely knowledgeable and expert in particular areas also tend to develop a fresh sort of naivety towards their work, not being afraid to ask the simple questions or explore such questions with others in ways that can re-orientate them particularly at times when they feel blocked. Creative people inject great discipline and structure into their work, but also paradoxically, bring a spirit of playfulness and lightheartedness to what they do. They combine reality with imagination, spend time talking and interacting as well as thinking and reflecting, are passionate about what they do but are also able to cast a colder more objective eye over their work and ideas. Essentially, they live with and personify paradox. They bring certain extremes to the way in which they work and play. In many cultures, we associate hard work with seriousness, discipline, objectivity, physical and mental energy and a certain amount of pain and sacrifice. And that may well be true for certain aspects of any dynamics of teaching as it is for any other realm of endeavour. But unless this is tempered with enjoyment, playfulness, imagination and passion the experience of hard work risks becoming a joyless grind – a site for stress, anxiety and burnout. Being a creative teacher is not about working yourself into the ground. It's about finding an engaging and exhilarating balance that engages both you and your students.

Crème (2003) argues that by being more creatively engaged ourselves, we can bring out the best of learning experiences in our students: 'we could try,' she suggests 'for a "creative criticality", a reflexive objectivity that evolves from engagement and connectedness rather than alienation and fear' (p. 276).

3.24 Promoting academic honesty

- Many students are unaware of the rules and possible sanctions associated with cheating at college or university.
- Addressing academic dishonesty and plagiarism should be less of a witch hunt (Slater 2006) and more of a process through which students observe mutual responsibility and accountability for ethical learning practices.

Colleges and universities appear to have become increasingly concerned about the issue of plagiarism and other forms of academic dishonesty. Chaky and Diekhoff (2002) identify many reasons why detecting and tackling academic dishonesty can seem an almost impossible task, citing such complex and multidimensional factors as greater access to information, competitive educational systems that place greater demands both on students and educators, large classes, some students' immaturity and lack of engagement, inexperienced instructors, mechanical assessment approaches, low likelihood of detection, high rewards for cheating, and greater grade performance pressure.

It may be, though, that plagiarism and cheating as a phenomenon have not escalated as dramatically as much of the current discourse seems to suggest, but rather that the possibilities now emerging, with increased use of information and communication technology, have probably changed the ways in which it manifests itself. Scanlon and Neumann (2002) report similar levels of traditional and on-line plagiarism among a large sample of students, and note that those who self-report plagiarism are likely to employ both conventional and on-line methods in the same way. Chaky and Diekhoff (2002) examined the personal variables of internet plagiarists, noting that 'copying and pasting' was often perceived by students as being a legitimate and acceptable research practice.

Moore and Murphy (2005) have also drawn attention to the fact that, despite sanctions associated with it, students may engage in plagiarism for a range of reasons, not all of which include the intention to deceive. Plagiarism can also occur due to innocence, accident, desperation or unconscious internalization of information. Other evidence suggests that issues of plagiarism and cheating are not fully understood by many students (Scanlon and Neumann 2002). If you detect plagiarism, don't automatically assume that students involved are being deliberately deceitful, regardless of how disappointed or annoyed you may feel.

Chaky and Diekhoff (2002) also note, however, that 'many [educators] fearing time-consuming appeals and even litigation, approach academic dishonesty cases reluctantly, and only in situations in which the evidence is overwhelming' (p. 910). It is understandable that teachers may be reluctant to get involved in disciplinary processes with potentially serious consequences for their students, and, even where they have a strong case, they may feel unsupported by their institutions. But it is also fair to note that it is often in the most authoritarian teaching environments, with little class communication, a lack of student support, and little feedback on assessment that academic dishonesty can flourish.

Plagiarism may be a symptom of deeper issues underneath the surface that must be dealt with. If you encounter it, treat it as an opportunity to learn more about your students, their needs, expectations, habits and values.

Academic honesty is part of an orientation that students should acquire on their journey through higher education. Maintaining a formative and coherent approach towards plagiarism can help teachers to create a learning climate in which academic honesty becomes a central value.

Best practice may include observing some of the following advice:

- Don't assume students know what plagiarism is, and recognize the struggle that is sometime involved in finding and being confident in their own academic voice.
- Develop and disseminate a clear policy that includes a definition, guidelines and disciplinary processes associated with plagiarism, and stick to it.
- Design assignments to both mitigate against plagiarism and help students

learn good scholarly habits (for example, you can request all references are a maximum of two years old, or give extra marks for perfect referencing).

- Give students a chance to explain their work in situations where you suspect they have been plagiarizing.
- Guarantee equity across the board, as we know the most powerful influential factors in academic dishonesty are peer-related contextual factors (McCabe and Trevino 1997). Slater (2006) advises teachers to come up with a tariff-like system that does not always tie you to set outcomes, but serves as an indicator of the seriousness of the misdemeanour.

If using anti-plagiarism software:

- Notify students (both in your syllabus and verbally) that you plan to use the software on a routine basis and explain to them what it does.
- Advise students to submit their own work independently, using the software. Provide some training in doing so, and if possible, a trial submission.
- Be aware of data protection issues (who has access to your students' submissions, how is their anonymity protected, and when the information is to be deleted from the system).

4

Exploring and using teaching technologies

Introduction • Examining your attitude towards technology • Playing the role of facilitator • Introducing your students to the technology you use • Sitting on the other side of the technological fence – becoming an on-line student yourself • Deciding what you will and what you won't do on-line • Keeping feedback and assessment in mind

Introduction

The following sections explore some of the key ways in which you can orientate yourself towards technology in order to enhance your teaching and promote student learning. Whether or not you are experienced in or confident about the use of teaching technology, this section should help you to explore your technology-related attitudes, orientations and actions. And it might help when you are considering decisions relating to the use of technology within and beyond your classroom contexts. Some teachers enthusiastically embrace all of the learning-related possibilities and potential that technology contains. Others remain silently sceptical about such possibilities – some even feel a sense of fear and anxiety when it comes to introducing new technology to their teaching.

Wherever you consider yourself to be on that continuum, this part of the book should help you to think about how you might consider, develop and exploit your relationship with technology. If you are one of the 'techies', the next few chapters invite you to take stock of your current approaches, consider your own use of technology, reflect on your successes and failures, and see what future options may be available to you. If you are part of the majority that embraces technology to the degree that it represents reasonably convenient, non-intrusive changes to your teaching strategy, this section will challenge you to think what else you could be using technology for that could make the difference between 'good enough' and excellent teaching. And if you are a technology-reluctant practitioner, this section might help you to extract some of the drama and hype from the issue of technology in teaching by exploring some simple techniques that might encourage you to get started.

Throughout this section we emphasize technology that supports good student learning rather than that which dazzles and overwhelms with 'bells and whistles'. Overall, whatever your current orientation to technology in teaching, this section should help you to explore technology as an effective and facilitative mechanism for helping you and your students to achieve your teaching and learning objectives.

4.1 Examining your attitude towards technology

- Many concerns and issues about teaching technology represent reasonable perspectives and are likely to be at least partially based on a rational analysis of your context.
- If you feel resistant to using technology in your teaching, it is useful to know where the main sources of that resistance lie.

Amid white papers, strategic plans, roadmaps, resolutions and reports, all of them emphasizing the increasingly important role of information and communication technology (ICT) in higher education, a basic dilemma emerges: teachers are expected ultimately to drive the change, but they often are not ready, supported or motivated to do so (see, for example, Guri-Rosenblit 2005). Pressures on faculty to become more technologically aware and proficient are increasing and come from a variety of sources including changing student expectations, institutional promotion and emerging strategies relating to ICT integration. Peer teachers may exert pressure by adopting technology themselves and passing judgements on what a 'twenty-first century' lecturer is supposed to be like. Regardless of the drivers, we make the case here that using educational technology can be ultimately beneficial for teachers.

We often perceive in explicit and implicit ways that many teachers have basic reservations when faced with educational technology. These worries can have both rational and non-rational influences. But they often manifest in similar ways, ranging from passive avoidance to active resistance. If you are in some way resistant to or concerned about the issues of technology in teaching, it is worth examining the source of your concern or resistance.

Perhaps it is based on one or more of the following common issues:

- 'I don't have the time'. The speed with which the field of educational technology is developing can seem prohibitive and time is one of the most commonly cited reasons that faculty give for not engaging in more innovative approaches to their teaching (Risquez 2006).
- 'I don't have the technical competence'. There is a learning curve associated with the use of any new technology. You may feel like many teachers do – 'digital immigrants', constantly trying to catch up, even with basic content authoring tools. More technically advanced features, such as on-line quizzes, digital video, conferencing tools and virtual learning environments (despite being increasingly user friendly) still require a good degree of knowhow. To make things worse, the jargon of technology specialists often ostracizes and frustrates.
- 'I don't see the point'. You believe that many of the promises of the so called 'e-learning revolution' such as unlimited access, greater interactivity and more engaging learning in mass educational environments (see, for example, Millwood and Terrell 2005) have failed. Perhaps it is your view that there can be no substitute for a good face-to-face class and that it may be better to spend money and energies reducing class sizes and increasing student/teacher ratios (see also section 3.7).
- 'Technology disempowers me as a teacher'. You are somewhat concerned about issues of security, needing to rely on external help, or not knowing what may happen if you try something technologically new. Perhaps you fear that using technology may also bring new cognitive demands and extra work overload. You may wonder if others will hijack your teaching materials against your will, or if someone other than your students will judge your teaching skills. Or you may share Noble's opinion (2002) that rationalization and cost-cutting on the part of administrators is the hidden motive behind ICT integration. These may be the factors that keep you loyal to more traditional, simple, conventional teaching environments.
- 'I see the point, but I can't be bothered'. Perhaps like many, you feel that your environment does not appropriately support teaching innovation and is more concerned with research outputs, despite general rhetoric that teaching excellence should be explicitly valued and rewarded. Perhaps you feel that you are not being provided with appropriate guidance and awareness in relation to educational technology, that your efforts to keep up with new developments are not acknowledged on your career progression, that the responsibility for implementing technology is not clearly distributed, or that the resources and infrastructure to do so are scarce and unreliable.

If you share any of these perspectives, we don't promise to prove you wrong, but rather we offer some positive suggestions for becoming more positively orientated towards technology in teaching. The next sections will guide, encourage and advise you on how to introduce technology into your teaching repertoire and to consider as Millwood and Terrell (2005) have done that the use of ICT in education can give rise to 'delightful and engaging learning inquiry' and can 'promote community, citizenship and democracy' (p. 195). Perhaps some of the following discussions will help you to consider how to open new, creative avenues for both your own teaching development and your students' learning.

4.2 Playing the role of facilitator

- Teaching technology will reflect and sometimes magnify underlying teaching values, norms and climates of the context within which it is applied.
- Technology is best utilized as a way of facilitating student engagement, empowering their own autonomous approaches to learning, and enhancing interaction among teachers and students.

It is possible to interpret the new technology buzz words ('e-moderating', 'e-tutoring', 'e-mentoring', 'on-line communities', 'authentic assessment', 'social construction of knowledge') as concepts that are all directly related to the role of human interaction, active learning and student engagement. Some claim that emphasis has shifted from seeing students as objects of teaching (coherent with traditional top–down educational relationships) to placing students at the centre of the teaching process, delegating to them some of the responsibility for their own learning. However, you may think that teachers are using technology just to duplicate content and control-based teaching styles. It is quite common to hear faculty members claiming (and perhaps you have thought the same yourself): 'If I post my notes, class attendance will drop'. While some research indicates that this does not necessarily happen (O' Reilly et al. 2006), such a prevailing belief reflects a conception that the classroom is a space for content delivery rather than for learning. Do you ever wonder if your classes are interesting enough? Do you think your students perceive a relation between what you teach and the development of professional skills? Would you say you effectively facilitate them seeing a clear connection between assessment and useful learning?

It may be that ICT provides a fresh opportunity for us to confront traditional teaching assumptions, helping us to embrace or at least consider new ones more readily, those that allow us to be facilitators of learning rather than controllers. It might be that the use of technology could help the profession to move closer to a more enlightened and empowering approach to teaching and learning in general.

Although technology can be a catalyst for new teaching approaches and improved class dynamics, it can also generate undesired outcomes and even reinforce teachers' worst fears. For example, using technology simply to tighten control mechanisms may create more rigid and inflexible approaches to learning. Teachers whose technical orientation promises or implies 24/7 contact with their class may become slaves to their own availability or just frustrate and bemuse their students. Teachers who are excessively focused on providing on-line content resources without clear guidance or purpose are likely to face students' cognitive overload and will continue to risk giving rise to surface approaches to learning. And those who rely too much on technology may impoverish their relationship with learners by imposing artificial restrictions and barriers to communication.

In order to integrate ICT as appropriately as possible, you should aim to provide the resources and support necessary and to optimize learner autonomy, helping them to develop important skills allowing them to make the most of the tools and techniques you are adopting. To operationalize this premise when developing a more technological orientation it is worth considering its impact on three different levels: organizational, social and intellectual. Organizational tasks include planning the learning process, providing students with the information and resources they need to guide their own construction of knowledge, introducing students to the tools and technology to be used, organizing the learning activities, and respecting the commitments established with the class with regards to communication or provision of feedback. Tasks related to the social dimension of learning revolve around the promotion of a student-centred and personalized learning environment, as far as possible in the context of widened access and mass participation. Finally, intellectual tasks comprise the provision of experiences that support the process of construction of knowledge, encouraging students to take different perspectives, selecting pertinent contents and favouring meta-cognition (that is, awareness of the learning process) and deep learning as a final result.

These tasks do not necessarily differ from those already occurring in face-to-face teaching contexts. When we see technology as a lever of effective teaching processes, an enabler of sound educational principles rather than an end in itself, we get closer to exploiting the most positive aspects of its potential.

4.3 Introducing your students to the technology you use

- Different students have different levels of technological proficiency, and you will need to install supports that allow all of them to access the technological and on-line dimensions of your course.
- In blended environments, where you combine face-to-face and on-line teaching, it is important to cross-reference these two arenas of learning. Regularly reference key events in class in on-line material or discussions. And mention on-line material during face-to-face sessions.
- Try to keep issues of access and support simple and reliable.

Teachers' responsibilities, challenges and opportunities in introducing students to technology are not always straightforward, particularly as student populations become increasingly diverse. Any one class of students can contain 'digital immigrants' and 'digital natives', those with easy access to and experience with technology and those without it. Even though a lot of current discourse suggests that students tend to be technologically fluent, it is important not to assume that all of them will be either familiar with or positive towards your use of technology. You are likely to encounter at least some resistance and disorientation, particularly among certain types of students.

Salmon (2004) gives us three categories of student orientation towards technology: a number of students can be defined as *swimmers* (they dive in readily, are usually willing to help others and are advanced in their awareness of technological alternatives and options); the *waverers* (arrive late and need encouragement to get started, but do well and become enthusiasts if appropriate help is provided); and *drowners* (who find it very difficult to get started or accept help, have little motivation to participate and dislike ICT).

Keeping these three categories in mind, here is some concrete advice on how to ease your students' (and your own) transition towards a wise and practical use of technology in your class:

S – Support
I – Inform
M – Moderate
P – Plan
L – Liaise
E – Empower

- *Support.* It is essential that you provide students with some degree of active support in the use of technology, especially to avoid the 'drowners' from going under. In order to achieve this: (a) make straightforward documentation available to students and refer students to it; (b) organize trials and spaces for safe experimentation, training sessions and demos; (c) facilitate spaces for discussion on the use of the tools (both in class and virtual spaces); (d) facilitate alternative means of contact in the event that students have occasional (or regular) difficulties in accessing virtual spaces; (e) try to ensure that enough ongoing support exists to help students access and use technology – avoid the sense of abandonment that students say they feel when expected to use technology and on-line resources that they cannot access (Concannon et al. 2005).

- *Inform.* Remember that 'out of sight is out of mind' and ensure your students are aware at all times what learning resources and activities are available on-line and how they are related to their final performance. Try to create constant links between what happens on-line and face-to-face. Make sure that information is effectively disseminated.
- *Moderate.* Learn the basics of computer-mediated communication (a good place to start is Salmon 2004). Help to create trust by promoting an enjoyable yet respectful interaction space, monitor and encourage on-line discussions, remaining vigilant of possible problems like lack of courtesy to one another or bullying. More frequent and explicit purpose setting, progress reporting and problem solving communications may be necessary. Do not become the slave of your discussion forum though, just check it and actively contribute a maximum number of times during a given week.
- *Plan.* Keeping in mind the pedagogical purpose of each tool and activity, plan your course carefully each week and introduce tasks gradually to your class. Do not overwhelm students with too many resources; rather challenge them with questions. Be alert and change as appropriate when innovations seem to become more of a hindrance than a help.
- *Liaise.* Do not support your students alone if you can avoid it. Most institutions offer some formal help at central or distributed locations. Don't hesitate to contact these about your concrete needs and problems, request training or handouts for your students, ask for advice in using particular tools and best teaching practices or propose an action research idea. Finally, peer teachers (both within and beyond your institution) are also likely to have encountered similar problems with their students and the tools you use and may offer you the best advice from your own perspective.
- *Empower.* While being aware of basic technical competency barriers, provide techniques to encourage students to locate and use on-line resources rather than general computer training. Very importantly, promote a social dimension of the learning experience and encourage your students to support each other, especially across the age spectrum. You can do this by creating virtual spaces for your students where they are expected to collaborate, or by allocating a 'swimmer' mentor to 'drowners' as suggested by Salmon (2004). We know, for example, that mature students have found interaction with younger students useful in navigating ICT demands, and that in turn

this has been a way to help them to integrate more effectively within the general student population (Rísquez et al. 2007).

4.4 Sitting on the other side of the technological fence – becoming an on-line student yourself

- You can understand, pre-empt and address students' problems with technology by having an on-line learning experience yourself.
- Signing up for and participating in an on-line course can help to avoid blocks in your understanding about how students interact with technology in the interests of learning.

Just as we have recommended the benefits of having an academic mentor, a 'technological mentor' is also a very useful ally to seek out. This idea is something that an increasing number of academics are buying into, as evidenced by the proliferation of communities of practice generated worldwide around the use of educational technology tools. Peer teachers may be happy to grant you access to their course sites, advise you against common mistakes and redirect you to the relevant support staff.

But one of the most useful ways of gaining an understanding of the pedagogical benefits and pitfalls of on-line or blended learning is, even for a brief period, to commit to enrolling as a student in a quality on-line programme, or a short on-line module. It may be useful to look specifically for a course on on-line tutoring, educational technology or the like, but any on-line or blended course will provide you with experiences and insights that can make you more responsive and focused in your efforts to build technology into your own teaching. Taster courses and demos organized by a teaching and learning centre or educational technology unit at your institution are also an option.

Being an on-line learner will have an informing and useful influence on your own technological choices. Becoming an on-line learner is illuminating and challenging: you are likely to gain insights that will help you to start focusing on how to work around the challenges that it poses, and to exploit the opportunities that it affords.

4.5 Deciding what you will and what you won't do on-line

- In striking the right balance when developing technology in teaching, it's useful to be pragmatic, at least at the initial stages of your strategy.
- Always focus on what provides maximum learning return for your students without overloading your schedule and don't be seduced by unnecessary bells and whistles.

Integration of ICT in teaching is not necessarily about discarding traditional lecturing styles in favour of an apparently more sophisticated mode of delivery. Instead, a balanced, realistic approach to educational technology should be critical and reflective, and should sit alongside traditional methods ensuring the most appropriate is used, both in terms of students' learning and teacher's time. As suggested by Berner (2004): 'instead of piling on the assignments that instructors must grade and making irrational promises to answer all posts, the instructor must design a course with a thought in mind: less is more'. 'Less is more' means quality over quantity, empowerment over spoonfeeding, deep learning over information transfer, and importantly, substance over style. In order to avoid ill-conceived approaches to ICT that transform you into a slave, it is important to consider and plan your approach. Students will also find it difficult to adjust to an on-line learning environment if you make things up as you go along, using tools randomly or chaotically, or if they do not clearly see the associated learning goals or rationales. Your chances of success are much greater if you think not only about the processes involved in developing and using the technology, but also about designing learning journeys. Littlejohn (2002) gets the teachers she trains to plan a student activity before choosing the medium for delivery, encouraging them to document it fully, first as a 'storyboard'. Only after this, does she introduce her participants to web-authoring tools. This image of a small group of practitioners gathered around a flip chart without a computer in sight reminds us of the essential need for teachers and students not to become overreliant on technology. Observe these ten guidelines about the use of ICT in teaching:

1 Clearly identify aspects of your teaching and your students' learning that could benefit from technological innovation (e.g. class communication, organization, formative feedback, project-based learning, etc.). Prioritize those that your students have highlighted, say, in your teaching evaluations.

2 Get concrete, informed advice on techniques and processes that can be

adopted for your needs. Frameworks like Conole and Fill's (2005) offer a good starting point to design learning activities on-line.

3 Explore what support and tools are available to you, and avail of training opportunities on a 'need to know' basis, in order to acquire concrete skills needed to face concrete teaching issues.

4 As much as possible try to benefit from maximizing the returns on your efforts and those of your students. Avoid investing too much time in mastering a new technology that has limited benefits or restricted applications.

5 Implement innovation gradually and on a small scale, and give students chances to 'play around' with the technology in unrushed, non-threatening situations (for example, in training sessions and trial on-line submissions).

6 Equally, 'play safe' yourself: design your materials and activities in a separate environment to the one you use for teaching and migrate them across. Back up your work as regularly as you can, use student demo accounts and test as much as possible before launching a new idea.

7 Set up (and negotiate with the class) the 'rules of the game'. Clarify the level of contact and moderation they should expect from you as well as the level of involvement expected from them and how this will be evaluated and rewarded; define appropriate communication channels; and specify the rules of 'netiquette' (the social conventions of computer conferencing).

8 Do some quality assurance work (for example, sort out access and usability problems, listen to students' first reactions to a new technological innovation).

9 Rationalize the support you provide to your students (for example, you might want to make it clear that class-relevant questions will be answered in the class discussion forum and not by email from/to the teacher or you might decide to explore peer review as part of a formative assessment).

10 Evaluate your students' perceptions of your technological innovation, what they learned as a result, and ask them for their ideas about how improvements can be made. Critically evaluate students' feedback, and change your use of technology according to positive and realistic suggestions only. Explain to your students why you have decided to change or to continue with a particular choice.

4.6 Keeping feedback and assessment in mind

- Linking students' technological engagement to formative or summative assessment may be a useful lever to motivate them to embrace and benefit from teaching technology.

- Opportunities for assessing student learning through technology should be utilized and, if used as data to feed more conventional teaching forums, can give rise to more effective use of face-to-face time.

Although the lecturer's enthusiasm is an important trigger for the students to engage with technology (Concannon et al. 2005), initial enthusiasm is usually not enough to sustain their motivation. A teacher may assume that by providing them with on-line access to learning activities and materials outside class time, students will become more involved in their learning experience, or that by opening an on-line forum students will automatically rush to participate.

Many students tend to think and act in quite economic and pragmatic terms (see Mathias 1980). When facing a new task, they may ask themselves the following kinds of questions: (1) What do I need to do this for? (2) Are the other students doing it? (3) What will happen if I don't do it?

A focus on assessment is one of the keys to embedding ICT in your class. In turn, the introduction of technology facilitates more evaluation than might otherwise be possible or practical (on-line peer reviews, digitized quizzes, surveys and project assessments; plagiarism detection, automated feedback provision, simulations, etc.). Automatic distribution and correction escalates the amount of assessment possible, making the administration process more reliable and facilitating opportunities for assessment 'any time, anywhere'. This is provided, of course, that the technology is robust and that students have easy access to it. More importantly, the relationships between educational technology, formative evaluation and learning can be symbiotic: the introduction of ICT can reinforce assessment in complex and enriching ways.

Research has found unique strengths in computer mediated communication as a medium for feedback provision, despite commonly acknowledged limitations like lack of non-verbal cues and danger of misinterpretation (Bierema and Merriam 2002). Also, for more introverted learners who may find face-to-face contact difficult and sometimes stressful, on-line communication can feel safer and less intimidating (McCormick and Leonard 1996).

When technology is deployed well, automatic and personal feedback can be combined in ways that enhance each other. For example, on-line assessment can be effectively used to provide a trigger for more detailed face-to-face feedback to students. In turn, testing conceptual understanding is likely to increase learners' chances of participation in face-to-face sessions, substantiate further teaching and evaluation, facilitate individual discussions with your students, follow their progression more closely, and encourage students to revise material on a more continuous basis than might otherwise be the case.

In the light of the importance of promoting learner-centred environments that promote deep, reflective and independent learning, it is worth exploring the possibilities that assessment technology affords in helping to sustain these criteria. Issues relating to assessment are dealt with in more detail in Chapter 5.

5

Interacting with the institution: managing time, tasks and expectations

Introduction • Professional development and preparing a teaching portfolio • Having a few golden rules for students and colleagues • Managing your head of department • Treating your CV as a working document • Knowing the regulations and keeping records • Managing meetings and follow-up.

Introduction

Like any job, teaching involves learning to manage time, to navigate organizational dynamics and to take charge of your own career development. This chapter explores how you can manage the parallel demands of your career development, your boss, your time and your working context, and explores practical steps you can consider when facing the organizational complexities that sometimes impact on your work at college or university.

5.1 Professional development and preparing a teaching portfolio

- Keep track of your teaching achievements, reflections and developments in an organized and structured way.
- A teaching portfolio should generally contain information and evidence under the following headings: your own reflections on your approaches to teaching, students' responses to their learning experiences led by you, peer observations and discussions about key aspects of your teaching, evidence of distinguished or excellent teaching and your teaching enhancement strategies.
- Teaching portfolios are often a requirement as part of a teaching accreditation process for higher and further education teachers.

In many further and higher educational contexts it is becoming the norm for new teachers to pursue an accredited programme in teaching. This is an emerging change in the traditional professional development practice of higher and further educational teachers, where expertise in one's discipline was the benchmark on which teaching careers tended to be defined. Now, being an accredited teacher is more likely to be not just desirable, but increasingly, a requirement. This means that planning your professional development is likely to require you to earn an accredited teaching qualification, if you haven't already done so. The ways in which you can do this will depend largely on the support that you get within your own organization and the options available to you.

Note that accreditation options, professional development routes and opportunities are progressing all the time, so keeping up to date with your options as well as with ongoing professional development opportunities in your region is likely to be well worth it.

Whether or not you are pursuing a teaching qualification, the teaching portfolio has become important for you to produce: if you engage in this task, it is likely to enhance your capacity to reflect on your practice (Moon 2004) and to provide evidence of your achievements in teaching for career development and review purposes (Morss and Murray 2005). A portfolio of your teaching is a way of documenting your experience, achievements and distinctions as a teacher in the same way as a more conventional academic CV documents research-related achievements by listing publications, grants and awards (Seldin 1997). However, in compiling a teaching portfolio, the literature (see, for example, Fry et al. 2000) encourages you to approach the task of teaching documentation in diverse, reflective and comprehensive ways, including for example the following features:

- Your own reflections on teaching (using teaching diaries, module-based portfolios and reflections on particular teaching interventions and their effects on your students).
- Your students' experiences of your teaching (using student evaluation of teaching survey data, focus group reports based on student discussions about your teaching or qualitative insights provided by your students).
- Peer or expert analysis of your teaching planning, design, performance or assessment strategies (using peer observation reports, expert analysis of your curriculum design and development or external examiners' evaluations of your approaches to assessment).
- Factual information about the range and volume of your teaching responsibilities.
- Evidence of teacher/student rapport.
- Other indicators of excellence such as teaching awards/nominations, national or international invitations to teach elsewhere, or scholarship in teaching and learning as evidenced by published work that focuses on pedagogy and teaching within your discipline.

Keep in mind that many of the other strategies and ideas presented elsewhere in this book can provide you with raw material for building an impressive and effective teaching portfolio. See, for example, our advice on keeping a teaching diary (section 1.10) and reflecting on and responding to student feedback (sections 1.2, 1.3 and 1.4).

5.2 Having a few golden rules for students and colleagues

- It's useful to be clear and candid with students and colleagues about your working preferences and habits.
- Write your own list of golden rules that students and colleagues should be aware of and communicate these clearly.
- Don't have so many rules that you risk becoming the resident prima donna, but do select rules of engagement that will help students and colleagues understand and respect your ways of working.

It's not a crime to have quirky habits and pet hates as a teacher. If you can't bear split infinitives or you are a general stickler for grammatical accuracy; if you have an objection to reading wordy essays that exceed guideline word counts; if you only meet students outside class on certain days; or indeed if you have any idiosyncratic likes/dislikes or features of your working routine that make it easier for you to function (or those that you simply prefer), that's fine. Just don't expect people to read your mind. Having a small number of 'golden rules' that are well communicated and widely known can allow your students and colleagues to support the way you work rather than fight against it. So Friday is your writing day. Put a sign on your door and tell people. If your organizational culture makes that feel like an impossible task, then you may need to embark on some more explicit negotiations with your boss or colleagues in order to feel adequately empowered to take charge of this aspect of your working life. Do what it takes to protect time for yourself that helps you to manage the many and varied professional pressures to which you have to respond. Most people who manage their careers successfully apply strategies that allow them to do this (see, for example, Covey 1990). If you want to go for a walk or a run at lunch time, you should be able to find a way to do this without undermining your professional contribution to your role as an academic. If you have particular requirements of your students when they submit essays, projects or assignments, then articulate them both to yourself and to them. Having a few golden rules both in managing your life and other people's responses to you is likely to create a more solid base on which you can work and deliver your responsibilities to yourself and to your students. Generate a list of 'golden rules' that focuses on what you like to do each week and what you would like your colleagues and your students to remember about your preferences.

5.3 Managing your head of department

- Your working relationship with your head of department is important, and it's worth being proactive and positive in your efforts to manage that relationship.
- It also pays to be straight with your head of department about your teaching preferences and expectations.
- Be assertive about your workload and the pressures that you may be working under, but also recognize and respect the pressures that your head of department is also likely to face on a day-to-day basis.

One of the most important professional relationships in any academic's career is with his/her head of department (HOD). The head of an academic unit/department is usually the lecturer's immediate line manager, with day-to-day responsibility for assigning teaching and administrative loads, as well as for facilitating the effective undertaking of these duties by providing appropriate resources, support and indeed mentoring. In many cases your HOD can also influence your research activities by controlling access to departmental facilities and resources useful in support of this research. At a more strategic level the head of department can influence your career progression through the ways in which he/she prepares annual performance review reports, proposes your appointment to various university bodies/committees, provides references in support of promotional applications, and otherwise creates opportunities and chances for you to develop.

If only for pragmatic reasons then, it is usually quite important to cultivate a positive and professional working relationship with your head of department. It is probably a good idea to be proactive about managing this relationship. Keep in mind that heads of department tend to find their own job demanding, pressurized and at times quite frustrating (Wolverton et al. 1999). When planning interactions and interpreting the actions of your own head of department, it is useful to consider the range of pressures and pulls that may be influencing them.

In this context, a proactive and positive approach to your relationship with your head of department is probably the best orientation to adopt. From a practical standpoint this kind of orientation might involve the following kinds of habits:

- If you approach your HOD with a problem or difficulty, present the issue in a clear, considered and succinct manner and try to present not only the problem but also spend time in advance considering one (or more) solutions that seem reasonable.
- Keeping in mind the number of people who report directly to your head of department. Try to differentiate between important issues that need his/her input and those that you should be able to sort out yourself with a little time and effort.
- Be candid with your head of department. Let him/her know the courses you would prefer to teach before the schedule is distributed. With regard to unassigned teaching, try to identify areas/courses you would particularly like to teach and where necessary, provide your HOD with a reasoned argument why they should be assigned to you.
- With regard to administrative duties, again try to identify duties that you would be particularly good at or those that you have a particular interest in and ask that they be assigned to you.
- If you feel a particular task could be undertaken within the department in a more efficient/effective manner or you identify some strategic initiative you feel the department should undertake (e.g. developing a new programme), be proactive in communicating these ideas and innovations to your head.
- Always be sufficiently prepared for meetings. Think about and prepare the meeting content in advance. In the context of meetings setting your future performance targets, always propose/agree to targets that are realistic and that fit as closely as possible to your personal career goals. Keep in mind that

on a pragmatic basis, it is generally better to outperform realistic target goals than fail to achieve overambitious ones.

These kinds of strategies and tactics are likely to be helpful in forging a proactive and positive relationship with your head of department. But they won't prepare you for every eventuality. Not all heads of department are consistently reasonable, fair, organized or positive in their approach to managing other people. Even the most well meaning head can sometimes get it wrong and, depending on their management style and yours, it is not unusual for conflict and clashes to occur. If you prefer direction and your head tends to be quite laissez faire, or vice versa, you may find interactions frustrating and difficult. It is useful to study the professional approach of your own head of department in order to formulate the most appropriate approach for you to adopt in response. In difficult situations it is a sensible precaution to acquire (usually from the personnel department) the recorded job description and responsibilities of a HOD in your institution as well as revisiting the job description/profile of responsibilities recorded in your own contract.

Most academic environments tend to operate quite a collegiate climate in managing departments and tasks, and many teachers tend to talk about their heads of department as supportive and protective colleagues who represent their interests within the wider organizational terrain (see Briggs 2001). We hope this is your experience too. However, where there are difficulties, clashes or where you sense that your head is placing demands on you that are excessive or inappropriate, you should have a good idea of the organizational processes in place that will help you challenge such treatment.

5.4 Treating your CV as a working document

- Your raw material for building and updating your CV can come from a wide range of possible sources, and should include a teaching portfolio (see section 5.1); research achievements, evidence of distinguished accomplishment in teaching, research or administration as well as basic facts about your career progression.
- Updating your CV regularly is a useful habit to adopt and it avoids the risk that you will forget important dimensions of your achievement as time elapses.

Academics are most often professionally judged/considered for career progression on the basis of a written CV. Despite this, many of us generate/update CVs only when under pressure to do so. Such updates are therefore often hurriedly prepared under time pressure, risking an incomplete or poorly structured document. There is obvious advantage to treating your CV as a working document and updating it regularly. It is often particularly useful to first invest time in designing an appropriately structured document. For many academics the three main headings should relate to research, teaching and administration/service, with the inclusion of additional subheadings as appropriate. The most convenient and comprehensive approach to maintaining an up to date CV is to set up an initial structured document and then to continually add subsequent achievements and experience as they occur. Even if work pressure prevents you from writing a comprehensive entry at any given time, a key word/sentence entry will ensure that the achievement is not forgotten when eventually updating the CV in more detail. It is also useful to keep a CV file into which evidence backing up CV entries can be retained, in case such information is subsequently sought. It is important too to tailor your CV appropriately for the purpose for which it is intended.

By keeping a core comprehensive CV up to date it is possible to generate variant 'specific purpose' tailored CVs, as required.

In many instances (e.g. academic interview/promotion boards) a proportion of those assessing your CV may not be technical experts in your academic area/field. In such cases it is particularly important that you contextualize the significance of your achievements within your area. Also, as you become more experienced and your CV gets longer, it is often helpful to prepare and present a single page summary of your most notable achievements at the beginning of the document.

Another beneficial effect of maintaining and regularly updating a comprehensive CV is that it allows you to reflect upon your professional efforts, achievements and general direction to date. This affords an opportunity for critical self-evaluation, which can help you devise future career goals/strategies.

5.5 Knowing the regulations and keeping records

- Having a broad familiarity with the key rules and regulations of your organization can help you to become a more trusted mentor to your students, can sharpen your practice as a teacher and advisor and can help you to ensure you act fairly and consistently towards your students.
- In keeping records about the application of organizational regulations you will accrue a number of useful benefits by being able to: (a) provide evidence that demonstrates a rationale for actions you have taken or decisions you have made; and (b) allowing you to check previous actions taken in similar circumstances, thereby helping to ensure consistency.

All educational institutions operate according to a set of rules and regulations. Make sure you have access to your organization's handbook/website of academic administration that sets out its academic regulations and procedures. These sources of information tend to be quite detailed, covering regulations and procedures relating to student enrolment, assessment, grading, progression and graduation. Regulations relating to both undergraduate courses and postgraduate programmes by teaching and/or research are usually included. Although not recommended as an engaging bedtime read, it is important to have a broad knowledge of these rules and regulations, and it makes sense to keep a paper/electronic copy of the most up to date version of this document close to hand for consultative purposes. Knowing the regulations is important from a number of standpoints:

- As a professional, your colleagues and students will expect you to have an understanding of these regulations and procedures.
- It is vital not to provide misinformation to students seeking guidance or clarification regarding an academic regulation/procedure. In addition to the obvious negative implication for the students, such an event could also damage your own academic credibility and even expose your employer to litigation.
- Knowing the existing regulations will allow you to contribute in an authoritative way to debates/discussions concerning future academic/institutional policy/regulations.
- A good grasp of the rules and regulations will help your one-to-one and group consultations with your students to be more strong-footed and assured. It can build your confidence as a teacher within your context and can enhance your students' orientation towards you.

In addition to institution-wide regulations it is likely that your academic unit/department has established a number of its own standard practices/procedures under these regulations. Again, the importance of being familiar with such departmental policies and procedures is self-evident.

While many academic regulations and procedures are relatively straightforward to interpret and perform, some (intentionally or unintentionally) leave scope for lecturer interpretation/discretion. The appropriate application of discretion invariably requires a degree of academic judgement, judgement that becomes sounder with experience. Newly appointed lecturers therefore may find it particularly helpful to discuss issues upon which they need to take discretionary decisions with more experienced colleagues.

In addition to knowing the regulations it is important for you to set up and maintain some sort of records system in which decisions, the rationale behind those decisions and any other relevant information are recorded. Although time-consuming and hardly academically stimulating, keeping appropriately detailed and comprehensive records can be crucial. Keep in mind, though, that no matter how well defined and observed, institutional rules and regulations cannot always cater for all eventualities, and remember the advice we provided in section 1.15 about the benefits of trust-based, collegiate and informal interactions.

5.6 Managing meetings and follow-up

- Meetings can become unproductive, purely ritualistic events unless participants engage and commit to their purpose and goals.
- Clarity and agreement about decisions arising from meetings is vital.
- Following up on meeting actions and committing to activating the agreements reached ensure that meetings continue to justify their own existence.

Meetings tend to be an inevitable feature of academic life, though teachers often question the purpose and effectiveness of many of them. If you find that your ability to do your job seems hampered by the number of hours you spend at meetings, perhaps it is time to take a critical look at this aspect of your professional life. On the other hand, despite the impact of communication technology, meetings can still be useful arenas in which to communicate important information, discuss, debate and develop important aspects of your work.

The effectiveness of meetings with your students and your colleagues is likely to depend on how these meetings are managed as well as how they are linked with other activities and followed up. Clarity about emerging decisions and agreements and the extent to which these are acted upon can quickly help shape our subsequent effectiveness and our professional reputations. Managing meetings well, in addition to reflecting positively upon your professionalism, ensures you make most efficient use of your time. Although some meetings are suited to informality (e.g. a quick, spontaneous discussion over coffee), many meetings are scheduled, formal parts of the academic calendar. It is worth engaging in a critical analysis of those meetings that you can and can't afford to miss, and planning accordingly.

Some of the more important pointers to successfully managing meetings include:

- *Adequate preparation.* Ensure that you have reflected upon the agenda item(s), gathered the appropriate background facts and that you have formulated your attitude towards the issues to be considered. Try to anticipate objections/obstacles to what you want and how these may be overcome.
- *Organization.* Where you are responsible for setting up a meeting, ensure that you attend to the nuts and bolts of organization – for example, inviting

all the appropriate relevant people, providing sufficient notice, booking an appropriate venue, making out an agenda and preparing any support material.

- *Chairing/facilitating.* All participants should concentrate on keeping meetings appropriately focused upon the agenda items, affording everyone the opportunity to make contributions while also not letting the discussion wander off in irrelevant or inappropriate directions.
- *Clarity.* As various agenda items are completed, it is important to make sure that all are clearly aware of what follow-up is required, along with who is responsible, the scope of the action, the timetable and how they report back. These points should be reflected in the written meeting minutes.
- *Follow-up implementation.* Follow up on actions agreed.

6

Assessment and evaluation

Introduction • Understanding why assessment issues make teachers feel uneasy • Enhancing assessment approaches by starting with simple questions • Considering the benefits of formative assessment • Being realistic about assessment • Useful orientations for giving written feedback • Key considerations when marking student work for summative purposes

Introduction

> The work associated with assessment depends on more than the linear communication suggested by process descriptions . . . it depends also on lateral communication, or unlegislated and undocumented interpretive practices. It depends on communication and negotiation, on ingenuity and serendipity, on judgement and insight – in short, on individuals taking the opportunities and constructing the mutual understandings that local circumstances allow.
>
> (Crook et al. 2006: 97)

Assessment is often seen as one of the most difficult, problematic and complex aspects of teaching (Gibbs 1999) and yet as many educational developers have pointed out, teaching cannot be considered without central reference to how learning is assessed and evaluated (e.g., Race 2001). Assessment is an exploration of the impact of many of the important things we do with students in higher education settings.

It has been argued that if we don't teach with an awareness of assessment options, issues and problems, we're missing out on getting to the heart of our teaching activity (Angelo and Cross 1993). Furthermore, it has been suggested that the more closely aligned and cross-referenced teaching and assessment are, the more likely we are to address problems in advance of their emergence, the more likely we are to deliver consistent and well integrated curricula, and the more likely we are to subject our teaching to the reflection and criticism that we know helps to nourish and sustain good learning and teaching environments (Bean 2001).

Many educational advisors recommend that rather than treating assessment issues in a post hoc, separate, divided way, assessment plans should be knitted into teaching strategies right from the very start (Jones 1999). This may involve a lot more work and sweat in the early stages, but it will really help you to plan, deliver and evaluate the effectiveness of your teaching in well integrated ways. However, we don't underestimate the challenges associated with a consistent, valid and learning supportive assessment strategy. There are contextual, political, resource and practice-based difficulties associated with achieving best practice in assessment (see, for example, Ecclestone and Swan 1999; Knight 2002).

Many teachers say they would like to assess in more effective, creative ways, but as soon as a good idea strikes them, they sense that the workload would be so great and prohibitive that they don't take their ideas any further. It's important to be pragmatic. It's not in your interest to become the sacrificial lamb of innovative assessment procedures – in any case the rewards may not be worth it for you. However, creative, innovative and effective assessment ideas don't always imply a backbreaking workload.

The following sections provide some practical guidance for the pursuit of good practice in student assessment, recognizing the inevitable resource and time constraints that prevail in many teaching contexts and are probably likely to prevail at least to some degree in yours.

6.1 Understanding why assessment issues make teachers feel uneasy

- Assessing student learning is not an unproblematic or straightforward process, despite the routine way it tends to be treated in educational institutions.
- Taking a wider view of the purpose of assessment involves recognizing that very few forms of assessment can provide a really precise measure of learning or performance.
- Assessment strategies, even those that are institutionally supported and

endorsed, are not always devised in ways that value and encourage student engagement in learning.

There is a lot of literature about assessment rationales, methodologies, approaches, philosophies and outcomes. For some excellent detailed treatments of key issues associated with assessment in higher and further educational contexts see, for example, Angelo and Cross (1993); Connors and Lunsford (1993); Brown et al. (1997); Brown and Glasner (1999); Cuming and Maxwell (1999); Black (2000); Heywood (2000); Cizek (2001). However, as a busy teacher in higher education with (it is likely) a wide range of other responsibilities and pressures, you may not have time to become encyclopedic about the wide range of material that is written, researched and has been disseminated about assessment. As Angelo and Cross (1993) point out, academics within their disciplines need to treat themselves (and be treated) as experts in the assessing, examining and evaluation of learning within their disciplines. As an academic operating within a particular field of expertise you are likely to know (or be in the process of coming to know) the boundaries, language, discourse and nature of your subject. And because of this, you are likely to be in a very good position to ensure that assessments you use are appropriate, worthwhile and supportive of particular learning goals. That's all very well in theory, but we know that many higher and further education teachers express at least some discomfort and uncertainty about their assessment methods, techniques and outcomes (e.g., Boud 1995; Knight 2002). Furthermore, even within the same departments and disciplines, teachers don't always share the same views as to what can be defined as legitimate learning goals (Cross and Fideler 1988). This sense of unease arises in part because assessing students' learning is not an exact science and that this lack of precision is coupled with the traditional requirements in higher and further education to attempt to express learning achievement in very exact ways. Examinations and essays are often given specific percentage marks, sometimes based on a broad intuitive sense about how the students have tackled the assessment. Even though strides have been made in explicating the nature of the required achievement of many assessment tools, the problems associated with assessment may actually lie in the underlying values, philosophies and assumptions associated with the purpose and functions of assessment for learning. Knight (2000) argues that assessment, rather than being viewed as a precise measure of performance, is better conceived as 'complex systems of communication, as practices of sense making and claim making . . . [and of] revaluing assessment practices as primarily communicative' (p. 285). This is a worthwhile stance. The pressures that you are under to give students a performance grade for demonstrating some level of achievement within your subject area, may not be based on a valuing of the implicit benefits of communication, engagement and discourse. Sometimes all you're required to do is fill in the box and put a tick or a cross beside identified criteria. All of these clashing priorities can make you feel, as someone charged with the responsibility of assessing student learning, quite unsettled about the process. One of the ways that you can overcome any uneasiness you feel about assessing your students' learning is to give enough time to reflecting on the goals of assessment and how we might achieve them, on exploring options and how we might activate them, ideas that are dealt with in the next section.

6.2 Enhancing assessment approaches by starting with simple questions

- Reviewing your assessment approach and strategy, either individually or collectively with other colleagues can start with the identification of basic principles, simple questions and fundamental goals.
- Adopting a simple approach to assessment rationales can help you to develop a clear, unambiguous and learner supportive assessment strategy that clarifies your own learning values and communicates these to your students in ways that empower and motivate them.

Assessing learning can indeed feel like a complex minefield, in which measures of performance, standards of achievement, evidence of understanding and demonstrators of learning outcomes become rather fearful ideas that we as teachers are never really sure we are doing justice to. Recognizing that there are no perfect measures of understanding, performance, knowledge or competence is important as is realizing that not everything can or should be measured.

A rather more pragmatic and reasonable approach to individual and group attempts to enhance assessment might be triggered by asking some simple basic questions, and using these questions as the basis of action orientated conversations about changing or developing assessment in areas that are within your realm of control:

- How can we design and use assessment to encourage better student work? Race (2000) points out that even when assessment is summative, it should always have a formative aspect to it. That is, on completion and consideration of the assessment a student should somehow have a clearer idea or a better strategy for either sustaining good performance or addressing areas of weakness where there is room for improvement.
- How can lecturers make more productive use of time spent on assessment? Teachers often talk about the time-hungry tasks that are associated with

grading, marking or evaluating their student assessments. They often report going into a sort of auto pilot daze (even though this makes them feel guilty) when marking student assignments, particularly when class sizes are big, and assessments are standardized and similar for each student. This does not always represent the best use of teachers' time. Are there assignment options that are less time consuming and/or more supportive of the learning goals of teachers and their students? Perhaps not, but it is at least worthwhile asking the question and seeing whether creative approaches to assessment can be more satisfying, engaging and effective than the traditional modes we may have inherited. An assessment audit that asks the question, at least creates the possibilities of finding better solutions than the ones we may be reluctantly living with.

• How can we ensure reasonable consistency in the grading of student assessments? We are sometimes forced to define quite fine-grained differences between students' performances on certain assessments and tasks. Where such differences are possible to identify and demonstrate, this might be quite warranted, but where they are not, perhaps broader bands of performance might be worth exploring, (e.g. pass/fail). Where many of us are marking, then the importance of clear templates and demonstrators of performance becomes even more critical.

(Adapted from Ecclestone and Swann 1999)

6.3 Considering the benefits of formative assessment

• Assessment puts your teaching to the test as much as your students' learning.

• Formative assessment does not have to be unrealistically complex or time-consuming. Simple interventions can help you and your students to become more aware and more reflective about the learning process.

Assessment decisions and practices impact on learning processes, class dynamics, students' stress and teachers' priorities when teaching. Evaluation exerts its influence in different ways depending on whether the emphasis is placed on learning itself (supported by formative assessment conducted during the course of the educational programme), or performance (deciphered through summative evaluation which is usually conducted at the end of the teaching process). Educationalists talk about formative and summative assessment as being qualitatively different from one another even though all forms of assessment can contain elements of both.

The purpose of formative assessment is to help students learn more effectively. Formative assessment is likely to be a somewhat less institutional-ized part of the learning process than summative types of assessment, and it tends to support student development in ways that students experience as being less threatening, more benevolent and interactive. Formative evaluation can occur without an emphasis on grades, marks or percentages. As Angelo and Cross (1993) argue,

> [formative] assessment helps . . . teachers obtain useful feedback on what, how much, and how well their students are learning. Faculty can then use this information to refocus their teaching to help students make their learning more efficient and more effective.

> (p. 3)

Also, as Kellough and Kellough have noted, 'the assessment component deals with how well the students are learning and how well the teacher is teaching' (1999: 417).

So formative assessment can be ungraded and anonymous, as well as simple and brief. For example, having students write a paragraph early in a semester can help you to get a quick picture of the basic writing skills of the class. Such an exercise can allow you to give useful feedback on a short piece of work and may help them to learn about conventions within your field, to improve their writing skills and to learn first hand about the criteria you associate with good learning. A small, formative exercise like this is also likely to have a pre-emptive and positive effect on subsequent summative assessments that you may set later in the semester.

Integrating opportunities for more formative assessment brings a teacher closer to aspects of teaching that are rich and enjoyable and transaction-free. You don't have to be an expert in assessment or have any special training to design formative assessments for your courses. Formative assessments can include many kinds of activities, most of them involve simply listening to or observing students' evidence of engagement with your subject. Don't under-estimate the time and energy any formative assessment innovation will require, but also keep in mind that if you scope out and plan the activities, you can achieve very positive results without an enormous or untenable time commitment. Here are two good examples of formative classroom assessment technique for which you can invent your own adaptations:

- *Minute paper.* Stop the class two or three minutes early and ask students to respond briefly to some variation on the following questions: 'What was the most important thing you learned during class?' and 'What important question remains unanswered?' Students can then write their responses on index cards and hand them in.
- *Documented problem solutions.* To become proficient problem solvers, stu-dents need to learn to do more than get correct answers. At some point they need to become aware of how they solved these problems and how they can

adapt their problem solving routines to deal with messy, real world problems. The documented problem solutions technique prompts students to keep track of the steps they take to solve a problem – to 'show and tell' how they worked it out. By analysing these detailed protocols – in which students have attempted to explain each step briefly in writing – teachers can gain valuable information about students' problem solving skills.

(Angelo and Cross 1993: 148 and 222)

These exercises have many versions, but each of them should have important commonalities. They can help you as a teacher to get a stronger picture of the learning experiences and milestones of your students. And, they can help students themselves to become more aware of and reflective about their own learning – something that many educationalists emphasize is an essential and transferable dimension of their education (Meyer and Shanahan 2004; Norton et al. 2004).

In order to use formative assessment regularly and with good effect, you may need to look at practical ways in which you can manage time more effectively inside and outside class. Technology may help you to do this (see also Chapter 4), but if technological innovations are not feasible there are multiple paper-based alternatives: self-assessment, group and peer assessment, learning logs or research diaries, collaborative design of assessment tasks, and so on.

Finally, constructive and realistic assessment involves a degree of adjustment to the characteristics of the students we teach. For example, research has indicated that those students who have less clear career plans do not always see the link between case studies, and are therefore less motivated by the authentic nature of the task (Concannon et al. 2005). Also, peer assessment is resisted more often by first year students than more mature learners, who tend to be more comfortable about assuming responsibility for their own learning and the importance of academic honesty.

Summative assessment can and should have formative characteristics. Unless students learn something important and interesting from all of their assessments, we don't utilize the opportunities that assessment affords. Even when you are testing students for the purposes of evaluating their performance and making decisions about progression and the quality of that performance, you are not restricted to narrow or single methodologies. Consider using a variety of assessment techniques and give your students some choice, reflecting at least partially, higher level skills such as synthesis and evaluation. Choices can go far beyond the traditional exam format and include techniques such as portfolios, cooperative research projects, papers, locally developed performance appraisals, simulations, reports from employers and so on.

6.4 Being realistic about assessment

- When planning assessment strategies for your courses, think broadly about the main aims associated with them and try to have a well developed idea about the different types of learning objectives you would like your students to achieve.
- Communicate these objectives clearly and regularly, demonstrating the links between the objectives and the course content.
- Have and communicate clear assessment criteria.

Teachers often experience some stress and anxiety about the ways in which they assess their students. Simple questions like the ones outlined in section 6.2 can help you to become more confident and focused about the ways in which you plan to assess student learning. It is also worth differentiating between types of learning objectives. What is your course aiming to achieve? Which of the following categories of competencies are you hoping your students will develop, and in what broad proportion?

- Basic academic skills.
- Discipline specific knowledge and skills.
- Contextualized knowledge and academic values.
- Work and career preparation.
- Personal development.

Being clear about the main learning objectives of your course in general, and of each formal learning session in particular, can help you to develop a realistic approach to assessment and, if well communicated, can encourage your students to engage in a discussion about the appropriateness of these goals from their perspectives, and to take ownership of their own learning strategies (Jackson 2004).

Recognize also that not everything can (or should) be measured (Docherty 2005). Pursuing 'good enough' assessment strategies can enhance the learner experience, rather than seeking an impossible precision that learning assessment simply cannot deliver (Race 2000). Good summative assessment should be reasonably valid, reliable, transparent, motivating and fair. But assessment should also be demanding enough to differentiate between levels of minimal competence and higher levels of achievement (see Bouriscot and Roberts 2006).

Also, it is much easier to get students engaged and motivated for assessment or examination by being as clear as possible about what you expect of them. Rather than being vague or ambiguous about what your assessment targets are, it is generally much more supportive of student learning to outline clearly to learners things like: what aspects of assessment you consider most important, how you are going to mark each dimension of an assessment, and what weight you are going to allocate to each part of a particular assignment or series of assignments. The more equipped a student is with the parameters, expectations and standards of an assessment system, the better they will orientate themselves towards a task, the less time they will devote to stressful guesswork, and the better they will generally perform.

6.5 Useful orientations for giving written feedback

- Differentiate between 'higher order' and 'lower order' concerns when giving written feedback to students.
- Remember that written feedback tends to need to be constructed more carefully than face-to-face advice – it can appear to students as being more hard hitting and intransigent – you may need to work to contexualize and explain it more carefully.

Teachers often need to give feedback to students in writing. Careful encouragement and constructive criticism are often much easier to deliver at face-to-face meetings. Written feedback is difficult both to give and to receive because it is disembodied from the person who wrote it. There is no comeback, or at least it feels that way. But where face-to-face dialogue on written work is not possible (and you will often encounter situations in which it is not), then it is useful to be aware of some of the most effective approaches to the provision of written feedback.

The following provides an adapted summary of advice outlined by Bean (2001) and might form a useful structure as you consider developing your own written feedback policy:

1 Comment on higher order concerns first, ones that seek to answer clearly and concisely, the following questions:
   - Does the written piece answer the question asked or focus on the assignment as it was defined?
   - Did the writer clearly generate his/her own list of issues/questions/thesis in responding to the assignment?
   - What are the key arguments made and are the arguments clear and of high quality?
   - Is the writing organized and structured effectively at the macro-level (i.e., clear, unambiguous beginning middle and end without repetition or

circularity, but including the reiteration of key ideas and the re-emphasis of key aspects of the piece)?
- Is the writing organized effectively at the micro-level (i.e., are the paragraphs well defined and laid out – does each address a clear but linked aspect of the overall series of arguments being put forward)?

2 Next comment on 'lower order' concerns:
- Are there aspects of the writing style that jar or are inappropriate? Is any of the writing awkward, clumsy or clunky?
- Could things be written in more elegant, 'cleaner' ways?
- Does the writing conform to grammatical rules?
- Are there any typos or spelling mistakes?

(Adapted from Bean 2001)

You will witness sometimes dramatic improvements in the written work of your students if you are up front with them about these kinds of questions in advance of their assignments. You may have concerns different from or in addition to those outlined above, but once your students know what it is you will focus on and when, they are likely to gain more proficiency in writing than might otherwise be the case. Assessing and responding to written work should ideally contain no surprises. Students should know what you think is important and how you expect them to grapple with your topic. Handing out a written statement on your key concerns in an assignment will create a much more stable set of responses from your students, it will improve their writing confidence and skill, it will cause them to enjoy writing more, and it will help them to 'train' their intellectual capacities in more directed and effective ways.

6.6 Key considerations when marking student work for summative purposes

- Remember that for students the assessment stakes can feel very high, and your decisions as an assessor of their work need to be sound and justifiable.
- It's important for you to have a sound marking scheme, to discuss it with other faculty and to keep records about how you applied it.
- Different disciplines have very different traditions and criteria when setting and marking exams (see Entwistle 2005). It is worth interacting closely with other teachers in your discipline to discover what these are.
- Design your summative assessments and exams in a way that reflects both the breadth and depth of the course.

For most disciplines a final written exam still represents the most common single mode of assessment employed. The exact format/methods pursued can vary and can include essay style questions, multiple choice, open book, case study-based, problem-based, in tray exercises or even a take away paper.

Setting a balanced and fair exam paper at the correct level is one of the most challenging tasks faced by teachers. Even experienced teachers sometimes get this wrong. Some issues to consider when constructing an exam paper include: (a) writing the questions in a clear and unambiguous fashion so that students understand exactly what is being asked of them; (b) providing instructions on the exam cover sheet; (c) setting questions that students can be expected to answer well within the time frame provided to them; (d) providing a balance of questions that truly reflect the syllabus covered and intended learning outcomes.

The structure of the exam paper and its individual questions deserves careful consideration. Assessment strategies fundamentally influence what and how students learn. Inclusion of an initial comprehensive multi-part question which draws on information from right across the syllabus, for example, will minimize student temptation to omit whole sections of the syllabus when studying/revising. Important from this perspective too is to ensure that your exam papers don't become too predictable. This can be increasingly challenging if you have delivered the same course over a number of years.

Setting questions that will discriminate between students is also a challenge. Straightforward essay-style questions that simply require a measure of lecture note 'regurgitation' are easy to set but are poor discriminators. The inclusion of one such 'surface' or 'easy' question can have advantages in terms of, for example, settling the students and providing a safety net for them. The majority of questions, however, should usually be more challenging and be capable of discriminating surface learning or memory from deeper and more considered learning. Questions that require an element of analysis, debate, synthesis or problem solving can be particularly effective in this regard.

Marking work, particularly for summative purposes, is a significant responsibility when one considers the potential effect it will have on a student's career. Marking final exam papers can be particularly challenging and stressful, as it usually must be completed within a short time frame. You may have more flexibility in the marking timescale for coursework, particularly if completed during the earlier stages of a course. However, from an educational standpoint it is desirable that this too be marked quickly and returned with comments to students. There is considerable evidence to suggest that the faster the feedback to the student the more likely it is to be of benefit to them (Bloom et al. 1971; Cross 1990). The points raised below may be useful in keeping practical considerations in mind when marking student work, particularly final exam scripts.

Pre-preparation of a relatively detailed marking guideline is an essential prerequisite. Typically this will include some form of list or guide to the main points you wish to see raised and an associated guide mark for each. Also included should be any more general criteria you intend to consider when marking, such as the overall structure of the answer or the extent to which you wish to see evidence of extensive outside reading.

The level of detail appropriate to a marking scheme will often be dependent upon the discipline involved. Very detailed model answers are usually possible to prepare for maths-based subjects, whereas a humanities examiner may wish to leave considerably more scope or flexibility. Preparation of too detailed or over-rigid a document can be counterproductive. Applying it rigorously to each exam script can be onerous and maintaining some examiner discretion is usually desirable, particularly if you need to adjudicate on any issue which falls outside the scope of the core marking template prepared. It is sensible also to consult with your departmental/college policy with regard to exam correction guidelines, and to keep well organized records.

Marking written work, in particular a large volume of work and in a tight timescale, is often mentally and physically draining. Try to be well rested and alert before you begin correcting and take regular breaks during the correcting process. A short walk, listening to some music or some other favoured activity can help to keep you mentally and physically fresh. Continued, uninterrupted correction is counterproductive and the associated fatigue increases the probability of marking errors or inconsistencies. In this regard, you can double-check your marking consistency by periodically re-marking a previously marked question. Also most find that correcting each single question at a time across all scripts can improve marking consistency.

Making notes on the margins of the scripts or coursework can help you (and the student) understand the marking logic if the script needs to be revisited later. Always check your institution's policy on making notes in exam scripts – as policies do vary. Another good practice is to double-check everything when adding up marks awarded and assigning a grade. Finally, keep an exam correcting log in which you can note reflections of the paper, specific questions and answers. These reflections can help you improve your examination skills and sharing of appropriate entries with students can help them in future exam situations. A log like this can provide excellent material for your teaching portfolio too.

7

Minding yourself: focusing on health and well-being

Looking for help when you need it • Switching off • Getting exercise • Eating wisely • Minding your posture, your breathing and your voice • Managing your own stress • Knowing when to say no, but keeping your promises

This section encourages you to focus on your own health and well-being within your professional life. Please note that we're not attempting to imply that academic teachers are a particularly unhealthy or unfit lot, or at least that they are any more unhealthy or unfit than the general population. However, we do know that there are pressures and challenges associated with teaching that carry certain risks and hazards and that could affect your health and well-being. For example, academic life can be sedentary and physically inactive (Dale 2004), and sometimes psychologically threatening (Chandler et al. 2002).

Implicit in the teaching profession is the assumption that teachers are role models to their students. If we are stressed, frazzled, overwhelmed, poorly nourished or otherwise physically or psychologically unhealthy, then we risk sending an inaccurate message to the people who we teach that suggests these are unavoidable occupational hazards. This is a myth that we should challenge not just in what we say to our students, but also in how we live. Besides, we have both a right and a responsibility to our students, our families, our friends and ourselves to stay in good physical and emotional shape. This chapter will help to provide some practical ideas for the effective management of your health and well-being. It may facilitate your own development of a structured approach to self-care. Being an effective teacher in the long term requires looking after your own needs and concerns as well as taking care of the needs and concerns of your students.

7.1 Looking for help when you need it

- Don't expect to be on top of every aspect of your teaching job all the time.
- Track your teaching year (say by consulting your teaching diary) to become practised at predicting times when you'll probably need help or support from colleagues or others.
- Become familiar with the services within and beyond your own organization that might be useful to turn to at times when teaching feels difficult, overly busy or otherwise pressurized.

Acker and Armenti (2004) have shown clearly how academic environments are characterized by an ever-growing set of demands that sometimes feels impossible to fulfil. For many academics, while the demands can feel great and overwhelming, the supports and resources to help them respond may be hard to find. Teachers report that particularly at certain times of the year, or at crucial times in their careers, things do get on top of them, at least to a point where support from someone else would be very helpful. It's not just a matter of effective time management (though that can help) or of pacing and managing and where possible delegating aspects of your workload (though where possible, this can be useful too).

It is also useful to adopt a mindset that makes it possible to get help at the times when you need it most. And while they may not be immediately obvious, there are supports in almost every academic environment that can lighten the load, or at the very least help to put things in perspective. Centres for educational development, staff development funds, trusted colleagues, informal work groups, curriculum development advisors or even work-based counselling services might all be able to provide you with crucial support at times when the going feels tough. Increasingly, academics do say that there are times of the year when they wonder how they are going to get through particular tasks or demands, and many of them admit to feeling that they could do with help, either in the form of moral or practical support. Be prepared to admit when you feel swamped and to ask for help. Don't try and soldier on letting the load crush you. Get into the habit of looking for advice, help and input, and try to pre-empt times in the academic year when you know that things are likely to mount up. Sometimes it's just a matter of an extra pair of hands when things feel really hectic, or someone to talk things over with if, for example, you're finding a particular teaching environment challenging or difficult. And, remember that there will be times in your life as a teacher in which you'll need particular help to make sure that you and your students don't suffer unnecessarily in the event of illness, family crises or unexpected difficulties.

Think of something that you are struggling with. Perhaps there's a part of a course you teach that you're not sure you understand fully yourself and you're worried that you're simply not able to teach it effectively to your students. Perhaps there's a persistent behavioural problem among one of your student groups that you feel unable to tackle. Perhaps there are resource problems that are preventing you from delivering your courses in the way you would like. Perhaps you're under pressure to publish research papers, but can't find the time, the confidence or the focus to get down to tackling this task. Challenges and struggles are very common experiences for teachers in higher education. If you keep your own struggles to yourself, it's less likely that you'll find a way to tackle them successfully. Using a trusted mentor (see also section 1.11) and sharing your anxieties and challenges with people who you know will treat what you tell them in confidence, will create a resource of advice and dialogue that will allow you to look at alternative ways in which you can address obstacles and issues that are or worrying you. You need to contain your anxieties to an extent – not everyone within university or college systems are the appropriate people with whom to share your worries – some may even use your candidness as a sign of weakness or incompetence. But if you have good counsel, you'll find that very few of your problems will be unique or previously unencountered. Looking for support can be both reassuring and practical in helping to identify possible solutions and to moving to another level of engagement with many of the challenging tasks associated with teaching in higher and further education. The teaching profession is potentially very rewarding, but it is accompanied by many pressures and demands that are sometimes difficult to respond to – look for help when you feel you need it.

7.2 Switching off

- It is your right and your responsibility to identify clear times in your life for switching off completely from your job as a teacher.
- Resting from work and being entirely disconnected from your students and colleagues will feed your ability subsequently to re-engage creatively and actively.
- Your brain (and your body) need periods of deep, profound rest.

When Cziksentimihalyi (1991) subjected creative people to qualitative study, he observed that while on the one hand they brought great physical activity both to work and leisure, they also created opportunities in which they could experience plenty of quiet and relaxation. In order to be creative it seems that we need to be able to switch off just as assiduously and completely as we need to be able to switch on. Total disengagement is a skill that sometimes takes practice. Mobile technology makes it easy for us to be permanently available to respond to the needs, queries, demands and pressures of other people. The research environment and the performance expectations in higher education means that as teachers in this context, there is always something else we should or could be doing. Down time increasingly feels like it's somehow not acceptable or legitimate (Cooper 2000). But research has shown again and again that unless we give ourselves total breaks from our work, we risk burning out and slowing down in the longer term in a way that is neither good for us nor for the organizations in which we work. Jensen (1995) shows that the brain itself (apart altogether from its jaded owner) needs periods of 'deep profound rest' allowing it to recharge its energies, so to speak, to forge new connections and to regenerate its ability to give rise to new insights. Unless we give our minds and our bodies the chance to recharge in this way, we may not be exploiting our potential as well as we could. This is itself a good enough reason to be unapologetic about taking breaks from work. During the normal rhythm of your life as a teacher, give yourself time for reasonable and rejuvenating preiods of time off. Make sure these breaks are complete and engage in something completely different from your work-related activities. Even between holidays, make sure you develop a habit of switching off your mobile phones, Blackberries, emails and laptops at defined times of your day and week. Unless you switch off fully to refuel and to rest, then it eventually becomes difficult to engage in your work with the enthusiasm and the energy that good teaching requires.

7.3 Getting exercise

- Join or set up a lunch time walking/jogging club; go to the gym or take up a hobby that gets you outdoors and raises your heart rate to a healthy degree most days in your week.
- Design an exercise programme that suits your lifestyle and level of fitness.
- Looking after yourself and your skills as a teacher can be much easier if you inject the ingredients of a healthy lifestyle into your work and life routines.

As we have said, teaching in higher and further education can be quite a sedentary business (Dale 2004). While many teachers expend a lot of physical energy in the process of teaching, a lot of the work associated with teaching (lesson/lecture preparation, the assessment and evaluation of student performance, the writing of reports and papers, the carrying out of research and analysis, the communication of ideas and so on) involve a lot of sitting around on chairs, peering at computer screens. Taking breaks from this work can also be a physically inactive experience. The lifestyle of the teaching academic doesn't necessarily require any physical exercise, so it is easy to edit this important activity out of the repertoires of your daily, weekly and yearly routines. Research now shows that cognitive functioning in any field is significantly nourished by physical fitness (see Fox 1999). Furthermore, being reasonably physically fit enhances your mental stamina and persistence, has a positive impact on your ability to make sound decisions, and improves your ability to achieve creative breakthroughs when facing challenging problems (Neck et al. 2000). In general, physical fitness is related to better decision making and higher levels of cognitive functioning – both of which are useful for teachers in higher and further educational settings (this is apart altogether from the basic truth that being physically fit is simply good for you and your overall quality of life). Making space for exercise is important. If you feel you don't have time, then maybe it is time to re-examine some of the other activities in your life that are preventing you from doing this. Getting fit is not necessarily radically time-consuming, and may not require more than 30 minutes in your day.

7.4 Eating wisely

- Boost your intake of Omega 3 fatty acids – Omega 3 fats are often lacking in a modern Western diet (Simopolous 1999), yet they have been shown to be an essential ingredient for enhancing alertness and mental agility. To take in more Omega 3, try eating more oily fish like mackerel, tuna or salmon.
- Keep blood sugar levels stable – avoid physical highs and lows by eating slow-release carbohydrates contained in porridge, apples, raisins, oranges and wholegrain bread.
- 'Track the energy rhythms of your day and respond with good nutrition: small healthy snacks eaten regularly throughout the day may be a useful strategy to help manage and maintain energy levels. And try to make healthy options the norm.

Holford (2004) is among many nutritional researchers who has demonstrated the effect of different kinds of food on your brain. In order for your thinking processes, your ability to articulate ideas and your capacity to think creatively and divergently to be at their best, it pays to take a look at your diet. Energy levels that are expended before, during and after delivering a lecture give rise to huge levels of variation in respect of adrenalin levels, metabolism and even blood pressure. Keeping sugar levels relatively constant can help you to deal with peaks and troughs of energy levels. Snacking on healthy, smaller meals during the course of a day can provide an antidote to the kinds of physical slumps that are often a part of teachers' experience.

7.5 Minding your posture, your breathing and your voice

- Good posture and breathing are important features of professional health in teaching.
- For good posture while sitting, position your legs hip-width apart, keep your feet flat on the floor and hold your back straight (but not flexed).
- Ensure that your computer screen, your desk and your chair are all positioned so that you don't have to strain physically to maintain focus on your work.
- Voice care is something that many teachers don't ever think about and yet in the teaching profession it is a particularly important consideration.

Teaching and its requisite activities can be bad for your posture and your voice, which themselves have a range of health and performance implications that it's worth being aware of. As a teacher in higher education you risk spending significant lengths of time slumped rather unceremoniously over a computer screen, talking for long periods of time to large audiences, or twisting to look at a projected image and then twisting back again to look at your students. You will pore over student scripts, sometimes for hours at a time, and during these kinds of activities, you are unlikely to find yourself maintaining any awareness of what these actions are doing to your voice and your posture. We know from extensive research that 'bad' posture can impact negatively on the health of your back and core, your voice, your breathing and your joints (Rosenberg et al. 2001). The wear and tear of bad posture can have long term health effects as well as immediate impact on the way you present ideas and how clearly you can be heard. How you hold your body, and the kinds of stresses you place on it, can have significant impact on your muscular-skeletal system.

Good posture is simple, but in order to get into good habits, you may need to spend some time concentrating explicitly and making yourself aware of the ways in which you tend to position your body when sitting, standing, teaching, studying, reading or talking. It may seem like a trivial thing, but studies suggest that just as bad posture presents professional risks to your health, good posture creates a range of subtle benefits that are worth pursuing. Some of the activities that help to develop good posture include yoga, walking, meditation, breathing exercises or classes in posture-related exercises (e.g., the Alexander technique). Many long established teacher training, education and development programmes support the idea that attention to posture is an important part of professional life.

Concentrating on your posture can help you to avoid fatigue, back pain, repetitive strain injury and other physical discomforts or problems. Watch out for your own posture and help your students to become aware of theirs by practising and communicating the healthy principles of sedentary posture.

Good habits with posture and breathing are also important foundations to help you care for your voice. The UK's Occupational Health Guidance for the Training and Employment of Teachers (December 2000) points out that:

> Teachers are one of the occupational groups most likely to present with voice disorders. Predisposing factors are poor vocal technique, vocal strain, inadequate voice projection and inadequate breath support.

You spend a lot of your professional life using and projecting your voice, sometimes in large spaces to many hundreds of people. Simple ways to care for your voice include drinking plenty of water to keep your larynx healthy, making sure you rest your voice regularly and avoiding voice strain. If you are in a teaching space where you feel you have to shout to be heard, then you need a microphone and your organization should be prepared to provide that for you. For more information about voice care, breathing and posture in teaching, see: www.voicecare.org.uk

7.6 Managing your own stress

- Be aware that stress is linked with emotional, cognitive and behavioural dynamics.
- Not all stress is bad – we need some stress to help motivate and direct our energies in particular ways.
- Look out for the signs of excessive stress and take steps to reduce or eliminate stress that damages your personal and professional life.

The definitions of stress fall generally into three main categories: some focus on how stress impacts on or is caused by what you think (e.g. stress is a perceived imbalance between demand and response capacity, under conditions where failure to meet demand has important consequences). Such cognitive definitions shed light on the notion that stress can simply be caused by a knowledge or a perception that what we are being asked to do is either too difficult in terms of quality or excessive in terms of quantity. A second type of definition of stress emphasizes how it makes us feel: thus if we define stress as, 'A general feeling of pressure, anxiety and tension,' we're focusing on the unpleasant emotional consequences associated with the experience of stress. Or if we define stress as something behavioural (e.g. 'A fight or flight response capacity to a threatening situation'), we're zoning in on the notion that stress creates a readiness in us to respond in particular and sometimes dramatic ways. Interestingly, the real experience of stress is likely to impact on us in all of these ways, affecting what we think, influencing how we feel and affecting the ways in which we are likely to behave. A moderate amount of stress can be quite good for us, giving us a shot of adrenalin to sharpen our performance or helping to motivate our actions and focus our attention. However, if stress levels become excessive then we can be paralysed by an inability to function, we can find ourselves overreacting to trivial issues simply because we feel we're dealing with so much already, and the quality of our work and our lives can suffer. Signals that we are under too much stress might include a sense that we're flying off the handle about things that we'd normally take in our stride, a feeling of being totally overwhelmed or of not knowing where to start at the beginning of each new task or day, a sense of hopelessness or panic. Most normal, high functioning teachers feel at least some of these occasionally. If such experiences are becoming the rule rather than the exception, it's definitely time to examine your workload, prioritize activities, talk to your head of department (see also section 5.3) or otherwise take steps to reduce and manage the stress levels that you are experiencing (Sarros et al. 1999). And part of what you may need to do is to learn how and when to say no – the timely topic of the next section.

7.7 Knowing when to say no, but keeping your promises

- Choose your promises to your students carefully, remember that you have made them and keep them as assiduously as you can.
- By doing this you will avoid a lot of frustration among your learners and you will reap a multiplicity of rewards.

Be aware of your commitments and your schedule. Learn what you can reasonably take on at different times of the year. Develop a rational capacity to say no when you know that what you are being asked to do will stretch you beyond reasonable limits. This will do you and your organization favours in the long run by ensuring that you continue to be able to work creatively and well, but not in excessive or unhealthy ways.

Students need to be able to rely on the things that you say you're going to do. It's better not to promise to photocopy a handout or to order something into the bookshop than to say you will and then fail to keep that promise. Of course you are a busy person, with lots of different responsibilities, and it is actually very easy to try to keep the demands of students at bay by saying that you'll do something or make something available or post something on the website – sometimes you'll be tempted to make these promises as you hurry perhaps from one class to another. Sometimes you'll do it as a way of avoiding lengthy conversations with learners at the end of a formal class session. It's natural to need to protect yourself from students' needs at least some of the time. But it's worth remembering that students rely on these promises and may value them much more than you do yourself. Make it one of your rules as a teacher: don't promise students you'll do something without first making a note of it so that you won't forget, and then delivering on that promise as soon as you possibly can. It seems like a small thing, but this kind of reliability can reassure your students and can provide benefits that go beyond the content of the promise itself.

Delivering on your promises simply improves your relationship with your students by building trust and confidence, and by making your students realize that you mean what you say. Furthermore, delivering on your promises almost automatically makes it more likely that they will deliver on the things that you ask them to do. Be careful though not to 'overpromise'. You can build in an understanding of what students can reliably expect you to do by managing their expectations and by incorporating a sense of this in the ground rules and learning contracts that you craft together at the beginning of your teaching/learning relationship.

Conclusion

This book has attempted to outline many of the key challenges and opportunities associated with teaching at college and university. We have presented simple ideas that we hope have prompted you to develop empowered and positive approaches to teaching and to outline the structures that you might use in developing effective teaching strategies in your context. Also, the literature that we have cited may lead you to explore some of these issues in more detail and more depth at key stages in your development as a teacher.

We hope that we have emphasized that while there may be many difficult and intransigent challenges in higher education, teaching and learning environments have low-lying fruit scattered everywhere. Small changes to teaching and learning orientations, tactics and styles can have big effects, and we have explored and signaled many ways in which you might consider availing of those effects or enhancing them.

With all of the developments in teaching and learning contexts, and with all of the progress in emerging communication and information technologies which provide promising avenues for teaching enhancement, it is still the nature of the relationship that we establish with our students that defines the future of education and its quality and effectiveness. We hope that you will find ways of nurturing and caring for that relationship in all of the teaching and learning interactions for which you are responsible.

Bibliography

Abbas, A. and McClean, M. (2003) Communicative competence and the improvement of university teaching: insights from the field, *British Journal of Sociology of Education*, 24(1): 69–81.

Acheson, K. A. (1981) Classroom observation techniques. Idea Paper, no. 4. Manhattan: Center for Faculty Evaluation and Development, Kansas State University.

Acker, S. and Armenti, C. (2004) Sleepless in academia, *Gender and Education*, 16(1): 3–24.

Adler, M (1984) *The Paideia Program: An Educational Syllabus*. New York: MacMillan.

Allen, L. (2002) Consenting adults in private – union and management perspectives on peer observation of teaching. Paper for LTSN generic centre. Available at: www.heacademy.ac.uk/resources.asp?process=full_record&section=generic&id=24 (accessed 5 April 2007).

Anderson, J.R., Reder, L.M. and Simon, H.A. (1996) Situated learning and education, *Educational Researcher*, 25(4): 5–11.

Angelo, T. and Cross, K.P. (1993) *Classroom Assessment Techniques: A Handbook for College Teachers*. San Francisco: Jossey-Bass.

Appleby, D. (1990) Faculty and student perceptions of irritating behaviours in the college classroom, *Journal of Staff, Program, and Organization Development*, 8: 41–6.

Armstrong, T. (1998) *Analysing Genius in the Classroom*. Alexandria, VA: ASCD.

Arthur, W.B. (1996) Increasing returns and the new world of business, *Harvard Business Review*, July–August, pp. 100–9.

Axtell, G. (2000) *The Pleasures of Academe: A Celebration and Defense of Higher Education*. Lincoln: University of Nebraska Press.

Barrington, E. (2004) Teaching to student diversity in higher education: how multiple intelligence theory can help, *Teaching in Higher Education*, 19(4): 421–34.

Banta, T. W. et al. (1996) *Assessment in Practice: Putting Principles to Work on College Campuses*. San Francisco: Jossey-Bass.

Becker, H. (1986) *Writing for Social Scientists*. Chicago: University of Chicago Press.

Beach, D. (1997) Symbolic control and power relay: learning in higher professional education, *Gothenberg Studies in Educational Sciences*, Vol. 19. Gothenberg: Acta Universitas.

Bean, J. C. (2001) *Engaging Ideas: The Professor's Guide to Integrating Writing, Critical Thinking and Active Learning in the Classroom*. San Francisco: Jossey-Bass.

Berhanu, G. (2006) Teaching in higher education: a personal account seen through a perspective of 'otherness' at a Swedish university, *Educational Research and Review*, 1(8): 272–85.

Berner, R. T. (2004) Less is more: designing and on-line course, *Distance Education Online Symposium (DEOS)*, 13(4).

Bierema, L. L. and Merriam, S. B. (2002) E-mentoring: Using computer mediated communication to enhance the mentoring process, *Innovative Higher Education*, 26(3): 211–27.

Black, P. (2000) Research and the development of educational assessment, *Oxford Review of Education*, 26: 407–19.

Blackwell, R. and McClean, M. (1996) Peer observation of teaching and staff development, *Higher Education Quarterly*, 50(2): 156–71.

Bligh, D.A. (1972) *What's the Use of Lectures?* Harmondsworth: Penguin.

Bloom, B.S., Hastings, J.T. and Madaus, G.F. (1971) *Handbook on Formative and Summative Evaluation of Student Learning*. New York: McGraw-Hill.

Boice, R. (2000) *Advice for New Faculty Members: Nihil Nimus*. Needham Heights, MA: Allyn and Bacon.

Boice, R. and Jones, F. (1984) Why academics don't write, *Journal of Higher Education*, 55(5): 20–34.

Bonwell, C. and Eison, J. (1991) Active learning: creating excitement in the classroom. ASHE-ERIC Higher Education Report No. 1. Washington, DC: ERIC Clearinghouse on Higher Education and the Association for the Study of Higher Education.

Boud, D. (1995) Assessment and learning: contradictory or complementary? In P.T. Knight (ed.) *Assessment for Learning in Higher Education*. London: Kogan Page, pp. 35–48.

Boursicot, K. and Roberts, T. (2006) Setting standards in a professional higher education course: defining the concept of the minimally competent student in performance-based assessment at the level of graduation from medical school, *Higher Education Quarterly*, 60(1): 74–90.

Brady, E. and Bedient, D. (2003) The effects of teacher presence on student performance and attitudes, *Impact 2003*, WebCT 5th Conference, San Diego, August. Available at: http://booboo.webct.com/2003/papers/Brady.pdf (accessed 5 April 2007).

Brew, A. (2003) Teaching and research: new relationships and their implications for inquiry based teaching and learning in higher education, *Higher Education Research and Development*, 22(1): 3–15.

Briggs, A.R.J. (2001) Academic middle managers in further education: reflections on leadership, *Research in Post-Compulsory Education*, 6(2): 223–36.

Brock, M.N., Yu, B. and Wong, M. (1991) Journaling together: collaborative diary-keeping and teacher development. Paper presented at the International conference on second language teacher education, City Polytechnic of Hong Kong, Hong Kong.

Brookfield, S. D. (1995) *Becoming a Critically Reflective Teacher*. San Francisco: Jossey-Bass.

Brookfield, S.D. and Preskill, S. (1999) *Discussion as a Way of Teaching: Tools and Techniques for Democratic Classrooms*. San Francisco: Jossey-Bass.

Brown, G. and Atkins, M. (1988) *Effective Teaching in Higher Education*. London: Methuen.

Brown, S. and Glasner, A. (1999) *Assessment Matters in Higher Education*. Buckingham: Open University Press.

Brown, G., Bull, J. and Pendlebury, M. (1997) *Assessing Student Learning in Higher Education*. London: Routledge.

Campbell, L., Campbell, B. and Dickinson, D. (1996) *Teaching and Learning Through Multiple Intelligences*. London: Allyn and Bacon, Simon and Schuster Education Group.

Carson, L. (2001) Gender relations in higher education: exploring lecturer's perceptions of student evaluations of teaching, *Research Papers in Education*, 16(4): 337–58.

Cashin, W. E. (1990a) Students do rate different academic fields differently, in M. Theall and J. Franklin (eds) *Student Ratings of Instruction: Issues for Improving Practice*, New Directions for Teaching and Learning, No. 43. San Francisco: Jossey-Bass.

Cashin, W. E. (1990b) Student ratings of teaching: recommendations for use. Idea Paper

No. 22. Manhattan: Center for Faculty Evaluation and Development in Higher Education, Kansas State University.

Cashin, W E. (1992) Student ratings: the need for comparative data, *Instructional Evaluation and Faculty Development*, 12(2): 1–6.

Chaky Lester, M. and Diekhoff, M. (2002) A comparison of traditional and internet cheaters, *Journal of College Student Development*, 43(6): 906–11.

Chandler, S., Barry, J. and Clark, H. (2002) Stressing academe: the wear and tear of the new public management, *Human Relations*, 55(9): 1051–69.

Chickering, W. and Gamson, Z. (1987) Seven principles for good practice in undergraduate education, *AAHE Bulletin*, 39(7): 3–7.

Cizek, G.J. (2001) *Setting Performance Standards: Concepts, Methods and Perspectives*. Mahwah, NJ: Lawrence Erlbaum Associates.

Clutterbuck, D. and Megginson, D. (2002) *Mentoring Executives and Directors*. Oxford: Butterworth-Heinemann.

Cohen, R.A. (1981) Student ratings of instruction and student achievement, *Review of Educational Research*, 1(3): 281–301.

Concannon, F., Flynn, A. and Campbell, M. (2005) What campus-based students think about the quality and benefits of e-learning, *British Journal of Educational Technology*, 36(3): 501–12.

Connors, R.J. and Lunsford, A.A. (1993) Teachers' rhetorical comments on student papers, *College Composition and Communication*, 44: 200–33.

Conole, G. and Fill, K. (2005). A learning design toolkit to create pedagogically effective learning activities, *Journal of Interactive Media in Education*, Portable Learning, Special Issue.

Cooper, C.L. (2000) *Industrial and Organizational Psychology: Linking Theory with Practice*. Lancaster: Blackwell.

Cosh, J. (1998) Peer observation in higher education – a reflective approach, *Innovations in Education and Training International*, 35(2): 171–6.

Covey, S.R. (1990) *Principle-Centred Leadership*. Toronto: Summit Books.

Cowan, J. (1998) *On Becoming an Innovative University Teacher*. Buckingham: Open University Press.

Crème, P. (2003) Why can't we allow students to be more creative? *Teaching in Higher Education*, 8(2): 273–7.

Crook, C., Gross, H. and Dymott, R. (2006) Assessment relationships in higher education: the tension of process and practice, *British Educational Research Journal*, 32(1): 95–114.

Cross, K.P. (1990) Teaching to improve learning, *Journal on Excellence in College Teaching*, 1: 9–22.

Cross, K.P. and Fideler, E.F. (1988) Assessment in the classroom, *Community Junior College Quarterly of Research and Practice*, 12(4): 275–85.

Cuming, J. and Maxwell, G. (1999) Contextualising authentic assessment, *Assessment in Higher Education*, 6: 177–94.

Czikszentimihalyi, M. (1996) *The Work and Lives of 91 Eminent People*. New York: HarperCollins.

Dale, L. (2004) Challenges for the older academic in balancing work and wellness, *Work*, 22(2): 89–97.

De Janasz, S.C., Sullivan, S.E. and Whiting, V. (2003) Mentor networks and career success lessons for turbulent times, *Academy of Management Executive*, 17(4): 78–82.

Dillon, J.T. (1988) *Questioning and Teaching: A Manual of Practice*. New York: Teachers College Press.

Docherty, T. (2005) Clandestine English: the subject without qualities, *The Cambridge Quarterly*, pp. 221–9.

Ecclestone, K. and Swann, J. (1999) Litigation and learning: tensions in improving university lecturers' assessment practice, *Assessment in Education*, 6(3): 377–89.

Elbow, P. (2000) *Everyone Can Write: Essays Towards a Hopeful Theory of Writing and Teaching Writing*. New York: Oxford University Press.

Elbow, P. and Belanoff, P. (2000) *A Community of Writers: A Workshop Course in Writing*. London: McGraw-Hill.

Ensher, E.A., Murphy, S. and Sullivan, S.E. (2002) Reel women: lessons from female TV executives on managing work and real life, *Academy of Management Executive*, 16(2): 106–21.

Entwistle, N. (2005) Learning outcomes and ways of thinking across contrasting disciplines and settings in higher education, *The Curriculum Journal*, 16(1): 67–82.

Everston, C.M. and Randolph, C.H. (1989) Teaching practises and class size: a new look at an old issue, *Peabody Journal of Education*, 67(1): 85–105.

Feldman, K. A. (1984) Class size and college students' evaluations of teachers and courses: a closer look, *Research in Higher Education*, 21(1): 45–116.

Fleming, N. and Mills, C. (1992) Not another inventory, rather a catalyst for reflection, *To Improve the Academy*, 11: 137.

Fox, K.R. (1998) The influence of physical activity on mental wellbeing, *Public Health Nutrition*, 2(3): 411–18.

Fox, N.J. (1999) *Beyond Health: Postmodernism and Embodiment*. London: Free Association.

Fry, H., Ketteridge, S. and Marshall, S. (2000) *A Handbook for Teaching and Learning in Higher Education*. London: Kogan Page.

Furlong, J. and Maynard, T. (1995) *Mentoring Student Teachers: The Growth of Professional Knowledge*. London: Routledge.

Gardner, H. (1993) *Frames of Mind: The Theory of Multiple Intelligences*, 2nd edn. New York: Basic Books.

Gardner, H. (1998) Are there additional intelligences? The case for naturalist, spiritual, and existential intelligence, in J. Kane (ed.) *Education, Information and Transformation*. Upper Saddle River, NJ: Merrill-Prentice Hall.

Gardner, H. (1999) *Intelligence Reframed: Multiple Intelligences for the 21st Century*. New York: Basic Books.

Gibbs, G. (1999) Using assessment strategically to change the way students learn, in S. Brown and A. Glasner (eds) *Assessment Matters in Higher Education*. Buckingham: Society for Research into Higher Education and Open University Press.

Gibbs, G., Habeshaw, S. and Habeshaw, T. (1984) *53 Interesting Things To Do in Your Lectures*. Plymouth: TES Books.

Gold, Y. and Roth, R.A. (1993) *Teachers Managing Stress and Preventing Burnout: The Professional Health Solution*. London: RoutledgeFalmer.

Goleman, D. (2000) Leadership that gets results, *Harvard Business Review*, March–April.

Goodyear, P. (2001) Psychological foundations of networked learning, in C. Jones and C. Steeples (eds) *Networked Learning: Perspectives and Issues*. Godalming: Springer.

Grant, B. and Knowles, S. (2000) Flights of imagination: academic women becoming writers, *International Journal for Academic Development*, 5(1): 6–19.

Grave, W.S, Boshuizen, H.P. and Schmidt, H. (1996) Problem based learning: cognitive and metacognitive processes during problem analysis, *Instructional Science*, 24: 321–41.

Gross-Davis, B. (1993) *Tools for Teaching*. San Francisco: Jossey-Bass.

Guri-Rosenblit, S. (2005) Eight paradoxes in the implementation process of e-learning in higher education, *Higher Education Policy*, 18(1): 5–29.

Hall, S., King, C. and Lawrance, B. (1996) Which way next? Sustaining innovative changes in units with multiple tutors, in J. Abbott and L. Willcoxson (eds) *Teaching and Learning Within and Across Disciplines*. (Proceedings of the 5th Annual Teaching Learning Forum, Murdoch University, February). Perth: Murdoch University, pp. 57–64.

Hammersley-Fletcher and Orsmond, P. (2004) Evaluating our peers: is peer observation a meaningful process? *Studies in Higher Education*, 29(4): 489–503.

Hansen, G. G. and Liu, J. (1993) Guiding principles for effective peer response, *ELT Journal*, 59(1): 31–8.

Hansen, J. and Liu, J. (2005) Guiding principles for effective peer response, *ELT Journal*, 59(1): 31–8.

Heywood, J. (2000) *Assessment in Higher Education*. London: Jessica Kingsley.

Hjortshoj, K. (2001) *Understanding Writing Blocks*. Oxford: Oxford University Press.

Holford, P. (2004) *Optimum Nutrition for the Mind*. London: Basic Health Publications.

Honey, P. and Mumford, A. (1989) *The Manual of Learning Opportunities*. Maidenhead: P. Honey.

Honkimaki, S., Tynjala, P. and Valkonen, S. (2004) University students' study orientations, learning experiences and study success in innovative courses, *Studies in Higher Education*, 29(4): 431–49.

hooks, b. (1994) *Teaching to Transgress: Education as the Practice of Freedom*. London: Routledge.

Ilgen, D. R. and Davis, C. A. (2000) Bearing bad news: reactions to negative performance feedback, *Applied Psychology: An International Review*, 3: 550–65.

Jackson, N. (2004) Developing the concept of metalearning, *Innovations in Education and Teaching International*, 41(4): 391–403.

Jackson, M.W. and Prosser, M.T. (1989) Less lecturing, more learning, *Studies in Higher Education*, 14(1): 55–68.

Jansen, T., Chioncel, N. and Dekkers, H. (2006) Social cohesion and integration: learning active citizenship, *British Journal of Sociology of Education*, 27(2): 189–205.

Jensen, E. (1995) *The Learning Brain*. San Diego, CA: The brain store.

Jensen, G. H. and DiTiberio, J. K. (1989) *Personality and the Teaching Composition*. London: Ablex Publishing.

Johnson, R. (1981) Student to student interaction: the neglected variable in education, *Educational Researcher*, 10: 5–10.

Johnson, R. (2000) The authority of the student evaluation questionnaire, *Teaching in Higher Education*, 5(4): 419–34.

Jones, A. (1999) The place of judgement in competency based assessment, *Journal of Vocational Education and Training*, 51(1): 145–59.

Joy, M. (2005) Group projects and the computer science curriculum, *Innovations in Education and Teaching International*, 42(1): 15–25.

Kellough, R.D. and Kellough, N.G. (1999) *Secondary School Teaching: A Guide to Methods and Resources; Planning For Competence*. Upper Saddle River, NJ: Prentice Hall.

Kezar, A. (2004) Theory of multiple intelligences: implications for Higher Education, *Innovative Higher Education*, 26(2): 141–54.

Kierstead, D., D'Agostin, P. and Dill, W. (1988) Sex role stereotyping of college professors: bias in students' ratings of instructors, *Journal of Educational Psychology*, 80(3): 342–4.

King, A. (1990) Enhancing peer interaction and learning in the classroom through reciprocal questioning, *American Educational Research Journal*, 27(4): 664–87.

King, C. A. (2000) *Systematic Processes for Facilitating Social Learning: Challenging the Legacy*. Stockholm: Department of Rural Development Studies, Swedish University of Agricultural Sciences.

Klein, P.D. (1998) A response to Howard Gardner: falsifiability, empirical evidence and pedagogical usefulness of educational psychologies, *Canadian Journal of Education*, 23(1): 103–12.

Knight, P.T. (2000) Summative assessment in higher education: practices in disarray, *Studies in Higher Education*, 27(3): 275–86.

Knight, P.T. (2002) Summative assessment in higher education: practices in disarray, *Studies in Higher Education*, 27(3): 275–86.

Knox, H. (2005) Making the transition from further to higher education: the impact of a preparatory module on retention, progression and performance, *Journal of Further and Higher Education*, 29(2): 103–10.

Kolb, D. (1984) *Experiential Learning*. Englewoods Cliffs, NJ: Prentice-Hall.

Kolb, D. A., Baker, A. C. and Jensen, P. J. (2002) Conversational Learning: *An Experimental Approach to Knowledge Creation*. London: Quorum/Greenwood.

Larsen, H.H. (2004) Experiential learning as management development: theoretical perspectives and empirical illustrations, *Advances in Developing Human Resources*, 6(4): 486–503.

Lea, M.R. (2004) Academic literacies: a pedagogy for course design, *Studies in Higher Education*, 29(6): 739–56.

Lillis, T.M. (2001) *Student Writing: Access, Regulation and Desire*. London: Routledge.

Lindblom-Ylanne, S. (2004) Raising students' awareness of their approaches to study, *Innovations in Education and Teaching International*, 41(4): 405–21.

Littlejohn, A. H. (2002) Improving continuing professional development in the use of ICT, *Journal of Computer Assisted Learning*, 18: 166–74.

Mann, S.J. (2005) Alienation in the learning environment: a failure of community? *Studies in Higher Education*, 30(1): 43–55.

Marcic, D. (1989) *Organisational Behaviour: Experiences and Cases*. Thousand Oaks, CA: Sage.

Martin, G. and Double, J. (1998) Developing higher education teaching skills through peer observation and collaborative reflection, *Innovations in Education and Training International*, 35(2): 161–9.

Mathias, H.S. (1980) Science students' approaches to learning, *Higher Education*, 9(1): 15–24.

McBrien, B. (2006) Clinical teaching and support for learners in the practise environment, *British Journal of Nursing*, 15(12): 672–7.

McCabe, D.L. and Trevino L.K. (1997) Individual and contextual influences on academic honesty: a multicampus investigation, *Research in Higher Education*, 38: 379–96.

McCormick, N. and Leonard, J. (1996) Gender and sexuality in the cyberspace frontier, *Women & Therapy*, 19: 109–19.

McGrail, M.R., Richard, C.M. and Jones, R. (2006) Publish or perish: a systematic review of interventions to increase academic publication rates, *Higher Education Research and Development*, 25(1): 19–35.

McMichael, P. (1993) Starting up as supervisors, *Studies in Higher Education*, 18(1): 5–26.

Meyer, J.H.F. and Shanahan, M. (2004) Developing metalearning capacity in students:

actionable theory and practical lessons learned in first year economics, *Innovations in Education and Teaching International*, 41(4): 443–55.

Millwood, R. and Terrell, I. (2005) Overview: new technology, learning and assessment in higher education, *Innovations in Education and Teaching International*, 42(3): 195–204.

Mishra Tarc, A. (2005) Education as humanism of the other, *Educational Philosophy and Theory*, 37(6): 833–49.

Mitchell, R. D. (1998) Learning through play and pleasure travel: using play literature to enhance research into touristic learning, *Current Issues in Tourism*, 1(2): 176–88.

Mitchel, C. and Sackncy, L. (2000) *Profound Improvement: Building Capacity for a Learning Community*. Lisse, Netherlands: Swets & Zeitlinger.

Moon, J. (2004) *Reflection and Employability*, no. 4 of the ESECT/LTSN Generic Centre 'Learning and Employability' series. York: Higher Education Academy.

Moore, S. (2003) Writers' retreats for academics: exploring and increasing the motivation to write, *Journal of Further and Higher Education*, 7(3): 333–43.

Moore, S. and Kuol, N. (2005) Students evaluating teachers: exploring the importance of faculty reaction to feedback on teaching, *Teaching in Higher Education*, 10(1): 57–73.

Moore, S. and Kuol, N. (2007) Retrospective accounts of excellent teaching, *Journal of Further and Higher Education*, 31(2): 133–143.

Moore, S. and Murphy, M. (2005) *How to be a Student: 100 Great Ideas and Practical Habits for Students Everywhere*. Maidenhead: Open University Press.

Moore, S. and Ryan, A. (2006) Learning to play the drum: an experiential exercise for management students, *Innovations and Education in Teaching International*, 43(4): 435–44.

Morss, K. and Murray, R. (2005) *Teaching at University: A Guide for Postgraduates and Researchers*. London: Sage.

Mumford, A. (1994) Four approaches to learning from experience, *The Learning Organisation*, 1(1): 4–10.

Murray, R. (2005) *Writing for Academic Journals*. Maidenhead: Open University Press.

Murray, R. and Moore, S. (2006) *The Handbook of Academic Writing: A Fresh Approach*. Buckinghamshire: Open University Press.

Neck, C.P., Mitchell, T.L., Manz, C.C., Cooper, K.H. and Thompson, E.C. (2000) Fit to lead? Is fitness the key to effective leadership? *Journal of Managerial Psychology*, 15(8): 833–41.

Noble, D. (2002) *Digital Diploma Mills: The Automation of Higher Education*. Toronto: Between the Lines.

Norton, L.S., Owens, T. and Clark, L. (2004) Analysing metalearning in first year undergraduates through their reflective discussions and writing, *Innovations in Education and Teaching International*, 41(4): 423–41.

Olivares, O.J. (2003) A conceptual and analytic critique of student ratings of teachers in the USA with implications for teacher effectiveness and student learning, *Teaching in Higher Education*, 8(2): 211–32.

O'Neill, G., Moore, S. and McMullin, B. (eds) (2005) *Emerging Issues in the Practice of University Teaching and Learning*. Dublin: AISHE.

O'Reilly, D., Doody, J. and Flood, M. (2006) E-notes and lectures: a mutual symbiotic relationship. Proceedings of EdTech 2006, the 7th annual conference for educational technology users in Ireland, Sligo, 25–26 May. Available at: http://ilta.dcu.ie/file.php/30/proceedings/assignment/12/488/eNotes_and_Lectures_A_Mutual_Symbiotic_Relationship.doc (accessed December 2006).

Orsmond, P. (1993) Peer observation of teaching, *The New Academic*, 6(2): 10–13.

Patterson, G. (1994) Student – administrator perceptions in a university setting, *Journal of Institutional Research in Australasia*, 3(2): 4–14.

Patterson, A. and Bell, J.W. (2001) Teaching and learning generic skills in universities: the case of 'sociology' in a teacher education programme, *Teaching in Higher Education*, 6(4): 451–71.

Perry, W.G. (1988) *Improving Learning: New Perspectives*. London: Kogan Page.

Petty, G. (2004) *Teaching Today*, 3rd edn. Cheltenham: Nelson Thornes.

Piaget, J. (1951) *Play, Dreams and Imitation in Childhood*. New York: W. W. Norton.

Price, P.C. (2006) Are you as good a teacher as you think? *Thought and Action*, Fall, pp. 7–14. Available at: www2.nea.org/he/heta06/images/2006pg7.pdf (accessed 5 April 2007).

Race, P. (2000) *500 Tips on Group Learning*. London: Routledge.

Race, P. (2001) *The Lecturer's Toolkit*, 2nd edn. Abingdon: Routledge-Falmer.

Ramsden, P. (2003) *Learning to Teach in Higher Education*. London and New York: RoutledgeFalmer Taylor & Francis Group.

Richards, J.C. (1990) The use of diary studies in teacher education programmes, in J.C. Richards and D. Nunan (eds) *Second Language Teacher Education*. New York: Cambridge University Press.

Richards, D. (2004) *What is e-Therapy?* Available at: www.cs.tcd.ie/~drichar/Portfiolo/Vision/index.htm (accessed November 2004).

Ridley, D. (2004) Puzzling experiences in higher education: critical moments for conversation, *Studies in Higher Education*, 9(1).

Rísquez, A. (2006) An exploration of faculty perceptions of a new learning management system (Sakai) in an Irish University. Paper presented at the 7th Annual Irish Educational Technology Users' Conference, Sligo, 25 May.

Rísquez, A., Moore, S. and Morley, M. (2007). Welcome to College? . . . Developing a richer understanding of the transition process for mature first year students using reflective written diaries, *Journal of College Student Retention: Research, Theory & Practice*, 9(2).

Rosenburg, B.J., Barbeau, E.M., Moure-Erasu, R. and Levenstein, C. (2001) The work environment impact assessment: a methodologic framework for evaluating health-based interventions, *American Journal of Industrial Medicine*, 39(2): 218–26.

Ross, J.A., Rolheiser, C. and Hogboam-Gray, A. (2002) Influences on student cognitions about evaluation, *Assessment in Education*, 9(1): 81–95.

Rutherford, L.H. (1991) Trying time: preventing and handling irksome classroom behaviour, *Instructional Development*, 1(2): 8.

Rymer, J. (2002) Only connect: transforming ourselves and our discipline through co-mentoring, *Journal of Business Communication*, 39(3): 342–63.

Salmon, G. (2004). *E-Moderating: The Key to Teaching and Learning Online*, 2nd edn. London: Routledge.

Samuelowicz, K. and Bain, J. D. (2001) Revisiting academics' beliefs about teaching and learning, *Higher Education*, 41(3): 299–325.

Santelly, M.I. (2005) From face-to-face classroom to innovative computer mediated pedagogies: observations from the field, *Journal of Interactive Online Learning*, 3(4): 1–14.

Salzberger-Wittenberg, I., Henry, G. and Osborne, E. (1983) *The Emotional Experience of Learning and Teaching*. London: Routledge & Kegan Paul.

Sarros, J.C., Densten, I.L. and Santora, J.C. (1999) *Leadership and Values*: Australian Executing and the Balance of Power, Profits and People. Sydney: HarperCollins.

Scanlon, P. and Neumann, D. R. (2002) Internet plagiarism among college students, *Journal of College Student Development*, 43(3): 374–85.

Schneider, P. (2003) *Writing Alone and With Others*. New York: Oxford University Press.

Scribner, S.A. and Anderson, M.A. (2005) Novice drafters: spatial visualisation development: influence of instructional methods and individual learning styles, *Journal of Industrial Teacher Education*, 4(2): 38–58.

Seifert, M. (2004) Understanding student motivation, *Educational Research*, 26(2): 137–49.

Seldin, P. (1997) *The Teaching Portfolio: A Practical Guide to Improved Performance and Promotion/Tenure Decisions*, 2nd edn. Bolton, MA: Anker.

Senge, P., Scharmer, C.O., Jaworski, J. and Flowers, B.S. (2005) *Presence: Exploring Profound Change in People, Organisations and Society*. London: Nicholas Brealey Publishing.

Sennett, R. (2003) *Respect: The Formation of Character in an Age of Inequality*. New York: W.W. Norton.

Shaw, G.B. (1950) Dedicatory epistle, *Man and Superman*. New York: Penguin.

Simopolous, A.P. (1999) Essential fatty acids in health and chronic disease, *American Journal of Clinical Nutrition*, 70(3): 560–9.

Slater, A. (2006) Hang 'em high! *Update*, November.

Sorcinelli, M. (1990) Dealing with troublesome behaviour in the classroom. Workshop and unpublished manuscript presented at Umass, Amherst.

Spandel, V. and Stiggins, R.J. (1990) *Creating Writers: Linking Assessment and Writing Instruction*. White Plains, NY: Longman.

Stein, S.J., Isaacs, G. and Andrews, T. (2004) Incorporating authentic learning experiences within a university course, *Studies in Higher Education*, 29(2): 239–58.

Stille, A. (2002) *Future of the Past: How the Information Age Threatens to Destroy Our Cultural Heritage*. London: Picador.

Strathern, M. (1997) Improving ratings: audit in the British university system, *European Review*, 5(3): 305–21.

Teixeira-Dias, J., Pedrosa de Jesus, H., Neri de Souza, F. and Watts, M. (2005) Teaching for quality learning in chemistry, *International Journal of Science Education*, 27(9): 1123–37.

Tileston, D.W. (2005) *Ten Best Teaching Practices: How Brain Research, Learning Styles, and Standards Define Teaching Competences*, 2nd edn. California: Sage.

Tinto, V. (1993) *Leaving College: Rethinking the Causes and Cures of Student Attrition*, 2nd edn. Chicago: Chicago University Press.

Vincent, A. and Seymour, J. (1994) Mentoring among female executives, *Women in Management Review*, 9(7): 15–20.

Winter, R. and Sarros, J. (2002) The academic work environment in Australian universities: a motivating place to work? *Higher Education Research and Development*, 21(3): 241–58.

Wiske, M.S., Sick, M. and Wirsig, S. (2002) New Technologies to support teaching for understanding, *International Journal of Educational Research*, 35: 483–59.

Wolverton, M., Gmelch, W., Wolverton, M. and Sarros, J.C. (1999) Stress in academic leadership: US and Australian department chairs/heads, *The Review of Higher Education*, 22(2): 165–85.

Woodhouse, M. (2002) Supervising Dissertation Projects: Expectations of Supervisors and Students, *Innovations in Education and Teaching*, 39(2): 137–47.

Zerubavel, E. (1999) *The Clockwork Muse: A Practical Guide to Writing Theses, Dissertations and Books*. Cambridge, MA: Harvard University Press.

Zinsser, W. (1988) *Writing to Learn*. New York: HarperCollins.

Index

Related books from Open University Press
Purchase from www.openup.co.uk or order through your local bookseller

---

THE HANDBOOK OF ACADEMIC WRITING
A FRESH APPROACH

Rowena Murray and Sarah Moore

The Handbook of Academic Writing offers practical advice to busy academics who want, and are often required, to integrate writing into their working lives. It defines what academic writing is, and the process of getting started through to completion, covering topics such as:

- Gaining momentum
- Reviewing and revising
- Self-discipline
- Writing regularly
- Writers' groups and retreats

Academic writing is one of the most demanding tasks that all academics and researchers face. In some disciplines there is guidance on what is needed to be productive, successful writers; but in other disciplines there is no training, support or mentoring of any kind. This book helps those in both groups not only to improve their writing skills and strategies, but, equally importantly, to find satisfaction in engaging in regular and productive writing.

Underpinned by a diverse range of literature, this book addresses the different dimensions of writing. The fresh approach that Murray and Moore explore in this book includes developing rhetorical knowledge, focusing on writing behaviours and understanding writing contexts.

This book will help writers in academic contexts to develop a productive writing strategy, not only for research monitoring exercises, but also for the long term.

Contents

2006   216pp
978–0–335–21933–9 (Paperback)   978–0–335–21934–6 (Hardback)

THE UNWRITTEN RULES OF PhD RESEARCH

Gordon Rugg and Marian Petre

A breath of fresh air – I wish someone had told me this beforehand.

PhD student, UK

This book covers things the other books don't tell you about doing a PhD – what it's really like and how to come through it with a happy ending! It covers all the things you wish someone had told you before you started:

- What a PhD is really about, and how to do one well
- The 'unwritten rules' of research and of academic writing
- What your supervisor actually means by terms like 'good referencing' and 'clean research question'
- How to write like a skilled researcher
- How academic careers really work

An ideal resource if someone you care about (including yourself) is undergoing or considering a PhD. This book turns lost, clueless students back into people who know what they are doing, and who can enjoy life again.

Contents
Preface – A challenge – About this book – Acknowledgements – So you want to do a PhD – Procedures and milestones – The System – Supervision – Networks – Reading – Paper types – Writing – Writing structure – Writing style – The process of writing – Presentations – Research design – The viva – Conferences – What next? – Useful principles and the like – Useful terms – Some further reading.

222pp   0 335 21344 8 (Paperback)   0 335 21345 6 (Hardback)

PERFECT PRESENTATIONS!

Peter Levin and Graham Topping

Made me consciously think about different aspects of presentations and furthermore gave me some very good ideas and 'little tricks' to keep the audience focussed.

MSc Management student

Will it be useful? Oh yeah! This gave me a lot of tools to do a good presentation and also to analyse other people's presentations and then improve my way of performing.

MSc Management student

An invaluable tool for anyone with a presentation to do in a class, seminar or in the workplace.

Perfect Presentations! helps students and professionals gain the skills and confidence they need to give an effective presentation. This lively, concise and to-the-point guide offers practical advice and tips not only on how to plan and prepare, but also on how to deliver the perfect presentation.

Perfect Presentations! is ideal for everyone who becomes nervous at the prospect of doing a presentation. Levin and Topping show the importance of knowing your topic area, structuring your presentation well, and building up a rapport with your audience. They offer many suggestions and exercises to help gain and develop these presentation skills.

- How to overcome your fears
- How to use body language and eye contact
- How to make your presentations audience friendly
- How to use visual aids

Contents

List of Exercises – List of Contents – Speaking to an audience with confidence and clarity. READ THIS FIRST! – Introduction – **Part One: Finding your voice** *– Training your body – Using body language and eye contact – Generating Energy –* **Part Two: Preliminaries** *– What is your brief? – Know your audience – Clarify your goals and objectives – How will you be assessed? – Observe other people's presentations –* **Part Three: Preparing your materials** *– Do your homework, think about your topic and decide your plan – Make your message memorable – Visual aids – Handouts – Prompts: index cards, script, notes, annotated printouts – Team presentations –* **Part Four: Thinking about your audience** *– Making your presentation audience friendly – Make friends with your audience – Speak with authority – Conquer your nerves –* **Part Five: Rehearse! Rehearse! Rehearse!** *– The benefits of rehearsing – Using your visual aids – Working as a team –* **Part Six: Last minute checks** *– Check out the room – Check out the equipment –* **Part Seven: Giving your presentation** *– Away you go . . . – Question-and-answer sessions –* **Part Eight: Giving your presentation** *– How did it go . . . What have you learned?*

2006   152pp
978–0–335–21905–6 (Paperback)